Flavors for Everyone:

A Guide to Raising Siblings
in a Special Needs Family

Barbara Lauer-Listhaus, Psy. D.

Flavors for Everyone

A Guide to Raising Siblings in a Special Needs Family

By Barbara Lauer-Listhaus, Psy. D.

© 2015 by Barbara Lauer-Listhaus, Psy. D.

Print ISBN: 978-1-68222-411-3

eBook ISBN: 978-1-68222-412-0

Contact the author at:

specialkidsdoc@gmail.com

To Alan, Joe, Jason, Maggie, Jessica, Henry and Kailey who give me the strength and courage to find my way down this unfamiliar path.

And to Jonathan for teaching us the true meaning of love.

Table of Contents

Introduction

Even under the best of circumstances, being a parent to several children in a household can be challenging. It involves a great deal of juggling in order to feel as if everyone's needs—including your own—are being properly met. Mothers and fathers strive to give each child equal quality time and attention, avoid "playing favorites," and foster loving and meaningful relationships. Despite your best efforts, however, sometimes it is difficult to maintain balance and peace among children of various ages with different interests and personalities.

Parenting a family that includes a child with special needs is even more complex. This is not an individual or even a two-parent undertaking but, rather, a family process that involves the siblings. The experiences of each family member will impact the entire group.

Just when you think your family is on a stable path, any one family member—and not necessarily the child with special needs—may require more care and attention than the others. At times, that care might involve arranging immediate intervention for one child and adequate coverage for the siblings or it might involve comforting a child whose emotional resources are spent. It might involve giving your spouse a much needed "time out" because he or she is experiencing frustration and stress; or it might involve asking a friend or relative to cover for you because you simply require time to yourself.

Life in a special needs family is always a delicate balancing act. With the increased incidence of children diagnosed with special needs, and specifically Autism Spectrum Disorder, parents are scrambling to find the latest intervention for their child. Simultaneously, they are inundated with the day-to-day experiences of managing their household and meeting the needs of all members of their family, especially the siblings.

Most of the research on non-disabled siblings focuses on their need to seek attention in the outside world, the harboring of animosity and anger toward the sibling with special needs, and the high incidence of mental health issues that arise. Often the mental health professionals who are conducting this research have a skewed point of view based on their involvement with the families that are facing crises and looking for immediate help. They rarely have the opportunity to see the many strong and resourceful families that are doing quite well despite the challenges they face.

As the parent of four children, including a son with special needs, and as a psychologist working with special needs families, I have come to understand this unique family experience from a different point of view. In my personal and professional encounters, I have found that many of these families face their experiences with courage and perseverance and, in doing so, teach their children to do the same. Most parents maintain perspective and remain optimistic when facing the daily challenges of balancing their family responsibilities, and many of the siblings they raise are extremely protective and concerned about their brother or sister with special needs.

Growing up in a special needs family can have great value. Children learn to become more independent and less self-focused. They learn to put the needs of others ahead of their own and appreciate all that they have. Children witness their sibling's ability to overcome challenges and become tougher and more determined themselves. They learn to face the outside world with intensity and courage. Most of all, they develop and demonstrate compassion, and a more mature understanding that life does not always turn out as planned.

Many families that include a child with special needs may be far too busy managing their hectic lives to analyze the value of their experience or may not have the opportunity to connect with or share advice and strategies with similar families. Through this book, I hope to help these families embrace their lives and feel empowered to find new solutions to the challenges they encounter. By conveying the meaningful lessons and important values that can be learned as a member of a special needs family, I hope to encourage other families—those with a family member who requires more support and attention, those facing other challenges, and those who are managing to get by—to see their situation and experiences in a more positive and inspiring manner.

All families will realize that their circumstances and emotions are shared. They will be comforted in knowing that there are no wrong actions and many good reactions that can benefit the family in any difficult situation. They will take the opportunity to appreciate the joy that each child provides and value the many memorable experiences that life has to offer.

This book was written to help those who are involved in raising a special needs family but will demonstrate to other families, by example, how to go "above and beyond" in facing any challenge that they may encounter.

As a parent, I have been in your shoes and have struggled with the same issues that all parents struggle with and worry about. Regardless of my professional training, credentials mean little when you are consumed by the desire to maintain the well being of those you love and cherish. My primary goal is to provide a sense of direction; a starting point for those who are in the earlier stages of finding their way down a difficult path, and an arrow pointing forward for those who may feel stuck.

Being a member of a family is a lifelong team-building project. It is also my goal to help parents recognize the benefits of working as a team member with a group of individuals who face a common challenge, and to teach their children life lessons of compromise, negotiation, and sacrifice for the good of the team. I want to help parents maximize the resources they may have available to them and to know when to seek outside resources when additional support is required.

Most of all, this book will show that when you set a goal for yourself and remain steadfast in your commitment to achieve it, you will discover that your abilities and talents are endless. As you become a winner in the game of life, *all* of your children will grow and thrive in ways you never imagined were possible.

Part I: A View from the Inside

Prologue: Flavors for Everyone

All children benefit from time after school to chill out and be themselves. Parents can benefit from this timeout as well. Before facing homework, dance classes, and therapy sessions, I found it helpful to spend quality time with my family in a child-friendly environment. After leaving work, I would regularly take my four children, including my son with special needs, to the local ice cream store where I discovered that in this relaxed setting, my children could express their individuality through flavor and topping selections and I, a busy working mom, could appreciate their company and distinct personalities.

I soon realized we could recreate the experience at home if I kept ice cream with all the fixings in the house year round. Best of all, my children's friends discovered this treasure and started coming over for play dates rather than avoiding our house and our son's disruptive behavior. Ice cream sundaes became the delicious way to invite the children in and, once they were in our home, they began to bond with all members of our family, often returning without checking the freezer.

One unexpected outcome was that many of our children's friends— those I thought were just visiting for the hot fudge and whipped cream— not only grew to befriend our son and embrace his unique differences, but have also maintained a relationship with him into adulthood.

Growing up in a special needs family can have great value. Children learn to become more independent and less self-focused. They learn acceptance, empathy, and appreciation for all that they have. Because our children witnessed their brother's ability to overcome his challenges and their parents' resilience and fortitude through tough times, they learned to face their own obstacles with greater determination. As adults, few challenges that they face overwhelm them.

The truth is that all children are *special* but they are each special in different ways, much like the ice cream they prefer. *Flavors for Everyone* highlights the importance of appreciating and making time for *every* child in a special needs family in order to promote personal development and success for both parents and children, and to create loving, long-lasting bonds among siblings.

Chapter 1: Our Family's Journey

My husband and I were cruising down the path of life, doing everything we could to advance our careers while simultaneously meeting the needs of our four young children, all under the age of eight. Everything about our life appeared to be normal. We were a two-income, hard-working, young professional couple juggling our jobs, children, and life in general. We became active in our community, volunteered on school committees, and were always busy. At the time, it seemed that all opportunities were ahead of us and there were no limits to what we could achieve, individually and as a family.

My husband is an ophthalmologist and I am a neuropsychologist. At the time, I was working in a rehabilitation hospital with children that were diagnosed with brain injury and neurological impairment. Imagine the irony when I soon came to realize that our child and our family would become a part of that special group of people.

Our third son, Jonathan, was not speaking or making any meaningful sounds by his first birthday and was not developing at the same pace as his two older brothers. In order to deal with all of the stress in our lives and remain emotionally available to our children, we would routinely convince ourselves that he was following his own unique path and would outgrow the problem.

This was around the time that our daughter was born. The delights and distraction of having a new baby also kept us from becoming too concerned about our son's delays. We were living our lives, doing the best that we could for our children. That "ignorance is bliss" scenario changed rapidly, however, as our son showed little progress in his language development during his second year. We—and Jonathan—were becoming increasingly frustrated by his inability to communicate and intervention became the obvious next step.

When we discussed our concerns with his pediatrician, the initial response was that all children develop at different rates and we should not compare him to his siblings. The doctor reassured us that it was normal for "boys to be delayed in language."

We willingly accepted this doctor's guidance because we were not ready to hear that our son had a disability that would impact his life. This occurred during the 1990s when Autism—its signs and its diagnosis—was not as prevalent as it is today. As a trained professional, I was certainly aware that Jonathan's language problems could significantly impede his overall development, but ultimately, the delay in receiving information about his condition actually helped us to more effectively face the many challenges that remained ahead. It helped us to remain focused on the present, finding a diagnosis and the right intervention, rather than becoming overwhelmed by the uncertain future.

As we proactively tried to unravel the mystery of our son's condition, the doctors and therapists we visited threw diagnoses at us including ADHD, OCD, thyroid deficiency, and Fragile X. With each new diagnosis, we took Jonathan for more tests and filled prescriptions for medications we hoped would fix the problem. But none of these medications was a cure and, in fact, several caused side effects that were more detrimental than the symptoms.

We were dealing with frequent devastation. One doctor told us that our son's delays were an indication that he had severe mental retardation and that he would never be able to function beyond the level of a one- or two-year-old child. She suggested that we explore opportunities for residential placement so that we could "move on with our lives and focus on our other children." But, in the same stubborn and determined way we faced other challenges, we were not ready or willing to accept that our son would not progress, and instead asked the doctor for additional weekly speech and occupational therapy sessions.

Despite my educational and professional training, and our ability to access resources in the medical field, at the core, I was a desperate parent looking for answers, and pushing for progress. I wanted our son to learn to read so that he could enjoy a book. I wanted him to learn to write so that he could communicate his thoughts to other people. I wanted him to make friends and have a girlfriend one day. I wanted the same things for him that I wanted for his siblings. Most of all, I wanted my family to be able to thrive, together and individually.

I found myself looking for comfort and support anywhere I went. I would speak to people on grocery store lines that would tell me about their relatives who did not learn to speak until they were three or four-years-old and were now doctors and lawyers. I wanted to believe those who said, "Einstein didn't speak until he was five-years-old." I tuned in to TV newscasts that featured experimental treatment for children with similar problems. I searched websites about new interventions and watched late night infomercials about toys that might teach my child to communicate.

As time passed and we were unsuccessful in finding a diagnosis or someone to direct our son's care, it became more and more evident that we were thrown into a job that would become the most important of our lives. And, it became obvious that we would have to be fast learners.

As I sat in the waiting rooms and offices of numerous specialists and therapists, I felt numb at times. Certainly, having been on the other side of the desk, I often felt like I was an observer and it took time to realize I was going to have to become a very active participant. It was like an out-of-body experience in which you know that this is real but it is so unfamiliar that you often feel as if you are acting a part in a play. You go through the motions and answer all the questions, but remain distanced from the process.

My three other children always brought me back to reality, however. They were young and needed my attention. They could not and would not be ignored. I forged ahead, doing what I thought would be right for each child, creating a sense of normalcy, and hoping for the best.

Like all the other moms I knew, I kept busy carpooling, attending Little League games, and preparing costumes for my daughter's dance recitals. After dropping the other children at school, I would take Jonathan to sessions with three different therapists several times each week so that he would have the intervention he needed to catch up. I tried to ensure that all my children would have the childhood I dreamed for each of them— the one I believed they deserved.

Even though I worked with special needs families and was surrounded by trained professionals, I felt completely alone. Despite a supportive family and many friends, there wasn't another person I knew who had the experience of raising a child with special needs like ours. I was shocked to discover that there were very few resources on raising a child with special needs and absolutely no guidance on raising the other members of my family, the siblings.

The professional literature and research I read painted a very bleak picture: that children raised in a home with a sibling with special needs would be deprived of their parents' attention and affection and would grow to feel resentful and angry that their parents were often distracted. They would feel helpless, hopeless, and depressed, and be more likely to face mental health issues as adults than their peers.

This scenario was not an option for my husband and me, and certainly not for my family. I was determined to maintain a balance and not only advocate for Jonathan's special needs, but for each of his siblings. I was determined to provide a cohesive and loving family experience for everyone.

I had worked with many families and if I could help them, surely I could help my own family. I was the expert after all, and if I couldn't do this who could?

Trusting My Instincts

As a psychologist, my career entailed supporting parents who were coping with a severely injured or ill child. I helped families understand the complexities of their child's condition and the impact on other family members. I listened to parents and helped them to cope and, ultimately, achieve some normalcy in their family life.

My approach involved encouraging the whole family—not just the parents, but also siblings, grandparents, aunts and uncles—to help and guide the injured, young family member's recovery. As I observed these family members relying on one another through very difficult times, I would identify the impact on each individual and help them to communicate their need for support. Working with these families taught me a great deal about how to cope when life takes an unexpected turn. Their strength and courage inspired me to set the same example for my family.

In the years that followed when I was on the receiving end, sitting in an office with my children and seeking the advice of other professionals, I had a different perspective than most parents. I realized that many of the professionals we encountered based their judgments and recommendations on the experiences they had with similar families. They were trained to remain objective and provide support but they really did not have an insider's view. I, however, had both.

Through these early experiences, I learned that parents know and understand their children better than many trained professionals, and they are certainly more committed to doing what is best for their children and their family. As a mother, I was the most invested member on the team. I realized that I, not the professionals, was responsible for directing my entire family's action plan when we became warriors in this same army.

In having my children's best interests at heart, I could intelligently analyze the whole picture and respectfully dismiss advice that I knew would not work for our family.

When dealing with my children, I became a keen observer and listener. I was able to see when one of them was troubled by our situation and needed time to talk it through. I acknowledged the differences between each of my children and would stop at nothing to get each of them the support and care that would help them to cope. My professional and personal experiences proved valuable. They allowed me to dismiss the guilty feeling that most parents face when they are inundated with suggestions and intervention.

The Value of Honesty and Inclusion

As the saying goes, "It takes a village to raise a child" and this is doubly so when raising a special needs family. We worked together as a family and learned from one another. Each family member's contribution was significant—and acknowledged as such—and there was never a time when our children felt that Jonathan's issues were more important than their own. We often came up with creative ways to include our children in their brother's care.

For example, after Jonathan was asked to leave several preschools due to his disruptive behavior, I hired a teacher who came to our home for two hours each day to engage Jonathan in preschool activities. Since my daughter was not old enough for school, she often participated in the activities as well. While Jonathan modeled his sister's behavior and learned to snap, cut, and color, in turn, our daughter enjoyed the adult attention and her role as an assistant to the teacher.

Another example was having story-time for thirty minutes every night before bedtime. The younger two children would select books that the older children would read aloud to them. In this way, the older children practiced their reading skills while the younger two learned to become good listeners. By reading each character's part in a different voice, my older son discovered that Jonathan would anticipate the changes and would become more engrossed in the stories.

Before they were old enough to know any other possibilities, our children became an integral part of the process and they each contributed, in their own unique way, to enhancing Jonathan's life. They were never required to take on these responsibilities and they were always praised for their contributions. Beyond any words of appreciation that we could express, they experienced their brother's own appreciation through his smile, his laugh, and his "thank yous," once he was finally able to speak. His responses motivated them to want to do more for him.

This experience of sharing and including my other children in Jonathan's care was valuable to them and taught me important lessons about myself. I learned that I had a lot more inner strength than I could have ever imagined, and my children learned that they were capable of helping someone else. I learned there was no situation that would defeat us, and they learned to work through a challenge. I taught them to see the world outside of our home and they learned the value of showing sensitivity and compassion to other people in need.

Our children impressed and inspired us time and again with their remarkable desire to protect their brother, and with their own creative solutions to the problems we encountered. We shared many proud moments watching our children work out difficult situations, whether within our home or in their personal lives. As I reflect back on the past and identify all that we learned, I am aware of the many ways that we have grown and will continue to grow because we were selected to care for this special child in our life.

Our Children and Their Special Needs Brother

If I were to share our formula for raising three siblings who are extraordinarily dedicated, loving and selfless, particularly in their relationship to their sibling with special needs, I would have to say that this is a process that involves many steps and stages. There is a part that is inborn and a part that comes from the environment.

Each of our children has innate traits that make them uniquely qualified to be the sibling of a child with special needs. We recognized those traits early on and provided the appropriate environment in which those characteristics could flourish. We also gave each of our children a great deal of love and respect, which allowed them to become better siblings and better people.

My husband and I demonstrated, by example, sensitivity and responsibility to one another, our family, our friends, and to the outside world. These characteristics were passed to our children, each of whom manifested these traits in a different manner. By offering a glimpse into how our own children grew to understand, accept, and consequently protect the interests of their special brother, I hope you will see what is possible for your own family.

Raising Special Siblings

Our first son, Joe, is thoughtful, attentive, and generous. In second grade, he received an award because he was very giving, and often shared his time and school supplies with his classmates. He is also protective and while he cares deeply for all of his siblings, he is especially fond of and concerned about Jonathan. Even as a young child, Joe was attuned to Jonathan's needs. Though shy and sensitive by nature, he seemed to be more outgoing when Jonathan was around.

At the age of seven, Joe asked to attend Jonathan's therapy sessions and he often asked questions. He would listen attentively to the therapist's reports about ways to engage or communicate with Jonathan and would practice these techniques with him at home. He would even find ways to adapt his toys so that Jonathan could play along.

When visiting a bookstore, Joe selected an interactive book with buttons that a child could press to make sounds at different parts during the story. Though Jonathan had limited communication skills and we were unsure whether he was processing the information he heard, Joe discovered that he could teach Jonathan to press each button at the appropriate point in the story. He would revel in Jonathan's laughter each time he heard the sounds and this became Jonathan's first positive exposure to the activity of reading. We learned that if we brought those books on family outings, time spent in the car and waiting on grocery lines would be more pleasant for Jonathan and anyone else around.

It was evident that Joe had certain personality traits that contributed to his behavior, but he also had many male role models who were extremely protective and loving. The most influential was my husband, who is a very dedicated brother to his own sisters, setting an example that Joe followed. But beyond this influence, I believe Joe's benevolent qualities flourished because Jonathan showed him appreciation and this reinforced their interaction.

Regardless of the origin, the outcome resulted in an incredibly concerned older brother. Contrary to the research I read suggesting that he would feel embarrassed or annoyed, Joe was extremely aware of the differences but truly did not care.

As the oldest, Joe had more independence and often enjoyed taking Jonathan with him on outings. He took it upon himself to take his brother to religious services, even when he went with his friends. When he learned to drive, Jonathan rode "shotgun" in the car, often joined by Joe's friends who learned to enjoy spending time with Jonathan. During the many nights that he didn't sleep and wandered around the house, Jonathan would often wind up in Joe's room, where he felt comfortable, secure, and always welcomed.

Years later when Joe went off to college, he called home every night before dinner to ask Jonathan about his day at school. Even though he didn't have a sense of time, Jonathan always knew when it was dinner-time because the telephone would ring. And, each conversation would end with some catch phrases – terms that they developed as their own unique system of communication. For example, when reminding Jonathan to behave at school, they would end the conversation with "So let it be written, so let it be done" (a phrase used in the movie *The Ten Commandments* that they watched together many times).

As adults, my children can anticipate a daily call from their father to find out about their day, and Jonathan continues to get his daily phone calls from his older brother. It seems that Joe passed the love and concern that he received from his Dad on to his younger brother. In observing this special bond, I experienced enormous pride. Joe has certainly played an integral role in caring for his brother and has made it clear to us, and to Jonathan, that he will always be available to care for him.

Our second son, Jason, who is technically our middle child, has rarely shown typical middle child behavior and has not expressed feelings of being neglected, less loved, or ignored due to birth order or as the sibling of a child with special needs.

From the outset, it was clear that Jason was very different from Joe, and he too has been a marvelous sibling to Jonathan. Jason was a more emotional child than his other siblings and expressed his feelings more openly. Even as a very young child of two- or three-years-old, he was extremely articulate and talked about everything he experienced. He was gregarious and enjoyed spending time with friends, but his brother Jonathan was always a part of those social gatherings.

As he grew older, Jason developed special routines and places that he shared with Jonathan. They were homebodies together. They enjoyed watching television and playing video games, but most of all they enjoyed each other's company.

When Jason was in middle school, Jonathan attended a summer program for children with special needs at Jason's summer camp. While many middle school children can be very self-involved, Jason was thrilled that Jonathan would be attending camp with him, and that their bunks were so close together. He spent his daily free time with Jonathan and often called us to report on Jonathan's progress.

Years later, I was impressed when Jason decided to become a counselor at the special needs sleep away camp that Jonathan attended. Though he had many options and could have spent time with his friends, he chose, instead, to spend his summers with his brother and other children with special needs. In fact, many of the children Jason cared for were more severely disabled and needed far more assistance with basic living skills than Jonathan required. His ability to put these other children's needs ahead of his own was quite impressive, particularly for a young adult.

Jason knew first hand the tremendous responsibility and patience this job required and was more qualified in some ways than the other counselors because of his experiences at home. He saw himself as a role model and believed he had a great deal to share with the campers and counselors. His experiences as a counselor resulted in long-lasting friendships with the other compassionate individuals, and some of those friends have pursued professions that involve caring for children and adults with special needs.

Each of these experiences enhanced Jason's awareness of the many skills and abilities Jonathan possessed that the other campers lacked. Most of all, Jason became more appreciative of our situation and the challenges we faced as parents taking care of a child with special needs. In fact, Jason met his wife through this camp experience, so our entire family has benefitted in immeasurable ways from his decision to spend the summer with his brother.

Our youngest child, Jessica, our only daughter, was born thirteen months after Jonathan. Unlike her older siblings, who were age six and four, respectively, when their brother was born and even older when we discovered his special needs, our daughter has shared her life with Jonathan since birth. I often believe that it was divine intervention that we had our last two children so close together, because once we were struggling with Jonathan's issues, we may not have had the time or been prepared to have another child.

It was also extremely beneficial that our youngest child was a girl.

From the time that she began to speak, Jessica has been Jonathan's translator, advocate, protector, and best friend. Even at three-years-old, she reminded the day care teachers that Jonathan had to be kept on a schedule during toilet training. Jonathan could not communicate well, but Jessica gave us a complete and thorough report of his daily activities. Our daughter shared every detail of his misbehavior, and eagerly informed us if anyone, including his teachers or caregivers did not show her brother enough attention. Forget about Nanny-Cam—we had Jessica!

Along with her very thorough reports, came a defensive presentation of any aspect of a situation in which she felt someone might have provoked her brother and triggered his unruly behavior. Rather than expressing jealously because of the extra attention he required, Jessica felt obligated to ensure that Jonathan was the center of everyone's attention.

She never behaved like a self-centered, unreliable youngest child, and in fact, behaved more like an older, more responsible sibling. From the time that she could speak, Jessica was independent and nurturing, advocating for her brother and for anyone who she believed was treated unfairly.

While carpooling Jessica and her friends to a birthday party, I overheard the group of five year olds talking about a classmate who did not like to share and often started fights during playtime at school. While her friends were content with the explanation that their classmate was "a bad kid," in her own terms, Jessica explained that this boy didn't play well with his peers because "his mom and dad gave him everything." She further explained "he is an only child so he's used to getting a lot of stuff and attention."

Even as a youngster, Jessica was aware of and could articulate the possible reasons and causes behind other children's actions. Her exposure to our family's many discussions about people's behavior—including Jonathan's—helped her develop this keen awareness.

As a teenager, she became active in programs working with other children with special needs, including a volunteer program that involved weekly visits to the home of a six-year-old boy with developmental delay. She became so committed to the young boy and his family that even when she didn't have scheduled visits, she would call to find out whether his mother needed extra help or if she could spend time with "her friend." He and his family were invited to Jessica's Bat Mitzvah and she proudly danced with him. This relationship matured over the years and Jessica continues to stay in touch with this family, even babysitting on occasion.

Over the years, she has channeled these skills into her other relationships. As an adult, Jessica is considered a very responsible and caring friend who is willing to help anyone in need and puts the needs of others ahead of her own. She is a good listener and her friends often request her advice and guidance in dealing with conflicts in their relationships. She has worked with other siblings of special needs children and developed a workshop to help them address the adjustment issues she faced as a young child. Jessica is pursuing a career in Occupational Therapy and plans to devote her career to working with individuals with special needs.

Our children do not fit the research about siblings in a special needs family. Clearly, there were many factors that influenced their adjustment, but a critical aspect was our family's ongoing commitment to each other and to helping other people. My children taught me so much over the years and continue to inspire me with their unwavering commitment to each other, and especially to Jonathan.

Moving Forward Together as a Family

When I first realized I was the parent of a child with special needs, there was no doubt in my mind that I could be a good parent to *all* my children. I knew that I would have to have more patience and find ways to balance my time among them, but I was determined to work together with my husband, to create a stable and nurturing environment.

In my psychology practice, I used a family approach to reassure family members that they were each important and could contribute to the recovery process. I encouraged family members to rely on one another through very difficult times, and taught them to communicate their need for support. I often suggested that families seek out whatever resources were available and rely on their own inner resources as well. These strategies and suggestions became invaluable to me when the tables were turned.

As parents, we did not allow ourselves to sit by passively waiting for things to happen to us or for us. We were open to all suggestions and willing to try anything, at least once. When there was no solution offered, we would come up with one on our own. We learned to recognize the problems that existed and that it was up to us to get over or around them. Most of all, through the process of discovering a course of action for Jonathan, we learned to trust our instincts.

As a couple, my husband and I worked together to make compromises. At times, one parent would take care of three children so that the other parent could have one-on-one time with the fourth. We had our children's friends over for play dates and when our children went to their friends' homes, we spent quality time with the others.

After dropping our older sons at school, and Jonathan at his therapy appointments, I would spend one-on-one time with our daughter in the waiting room, in the car, or at a park. When my daughter went in for her nap, I would work with Jonathan on the home assignments from the therapists before picking up my other children from school. From there, we would proceed to afterschool activities of tennis lessons, gymnastics and ballet. I limited each child to one afterschool activity at a time, so that they would appreciate the activity, and I would not be overwhelmed with an unrealistic schedule.

Often, I would bring along toys and travel games so that they could play together while waiting for their sibling to complete his or her designated activity. If I was organized and well prepared, they would be less likely to decompress and end up in a battle with me or with one another. I knew the location of the closest playground to each of the sport fields in our neighborhood in case a child needed a diversion while their sibling was finishing a game. Aside from maintaining the peace, the positive moments they shared while their other siblings were engaged in activities would go a long way in promoting my children's relationships with each other later on in life.

As we went through our daily routine, each of my children would benefit from the time and attention that was focused on them whether through quality time with us or at afterschool activities. The opportunity to explore other interests helped them learn new skills and to identify their talents. It gave me the opportunity to focus on the accomplishments of each child, and each child's self esteem was enhanced through their individual accomplishments.

None of us knows how the future will turn out. Life is about turning the page everyday and finding out about the next adventure. And, as was the case for us and for all of our children, the uncertainty allowed us to remain optimistic as we got through each day, living and enjoying life "in the moment." Our children learned that every day is different, and that each new experience requires adaptation since things are always changing.

And, perhaps most of all, we have managed to maintain our sense of humor and enjoy many laughs together.

In the end, the most essential aspect of our success was that we kept moving forward, in a positive direction, always hoping for a better tomorrow. As long as we maintained a bright and upbeat outlook, our children had a similar belief about their own futures.

Another factor in our success was having other important people in our lives, the extended family members and friends, who opened their hearts to us. Though, at first, we resisted the support and tried to do everything on our own, we were extremely fortunate to receive comfort and inspiration from many caring professionals and friends. These important people not only offered words of reassurance, but also personally showed up to lend a hand, so that we could take personal time to replenish or give each of our children a little more one-to-one time. Through building this community, we shared an enriched life together. Most of all, each member of our circle served as a role model to our children, helping them to become better people.

From childhood through young adulthood, we continued to frequent the ice cream store as a family, adding many other special family outings to our memories. These experiences have enhanced our bond since they required new and creative ways to include Jonathan, which enriched his and, ultimately, our growth as a family and a team.

I could not have imagined myself seeing this in a positive light when we first began this journey, but, as our family helped our son to grow and succeed, we all achieved our own personal best. I can honesty say that we are better off, perhaps the best we can be, because of all that we have endured and accomplished together.

Part II: Navigating the World of the Special Needs Family

Chapter 2: Understanding the Special Needs Family

As the parent of a child with special needs, you often ask the question, "Why?" *Why isn't my child doing things that the other children his age can do? Why isn't he or she learning to speak or walk at the same time that his siblings did? Why can't I find someone who can tell me what's wrong? Why did this happen to my child? Why did this happen to our family?*

You are not alone. All parents ask these questions once they realize that their child is different. Once a professional makes a confirmed diagnosis, these whys—and the feelings associated with them—reverberate throughout the family. Lives are forever changed in profound ways and it's reasonable to want an explanation. Unfortunately, for many of us, there are no easy answers and these questions will continue to resurface as you encounter future adversities and disappointments.

The responsibility of taking care of a child with special needs may often be a burden to you, but what may be less noticeable, are the ways in which this can impact other aspects of your life, especially your relationship with your other children.

If you endeavor to develop a strong bond with each of your children, they will look to you for psychological and emotional support throughout their lives and respect your guidance. This will require adapting to each child's unique personality and communication style, but it will be satisfying to watch them all grow, individually, into capable adults.

Though managing a large family can be challenging for any parent, for the parents of a child with special needs, handling the many needs of your growing family while juggling the responsibilities of taking care of a child who needs help with the simplest tasks, requires more energy and competence.

The concept of multitasking is far more complex than in other families. It involves making yourself available to children who are the same age but have varying levels of independence and self-sufficiency. As such, you often feel pulled in many different directions both physically and emotionally. Learning to take everything one day at a time will help to temper your stress and allow you to observe the joy of small accomplishments—your children's and your own.

Shared Emotions and Concerns

There are common emotions and experiences that all members of a special needs family share. These include:

- Coming to terms with a diagnosis
- Dealing with the guilt
- Feeling sad, helpless, and hopeless
- Feeling isolated and disconnected from other families
- Feeling burdened and overwhelmed
- Feeling angry and frustrated
- Feeling embarrassed
- Dealing with a loss of expectations and uncertainty about the future
- Fearing ostracism or bullying toward your children
- Experiencing a desire for balance and control

Once families are aware of their mutual emotions and concerns, they can begin to share their feelings with each other. As they unify in their loss of expectations, their fears, and their hopes for the future, together, family members, can reflect on and embrace their unique "new normal."

Family Dynamics

As a result of prior experiences, individual personalities, and the pressures and circumstances they may be experiencing, each family member is unique and their experiences are their own. As family members relate to one another, the chemistry that exists between them is distinct and may change over time.

Psychologists often refer to the relationships that exist between family members as the *family dynamic*, reflecting the fact that the family is a system that involves many individuals with different personalities that impact one another through their interactions. This term is especially relevant for the special needs family because it refers to a group of people that is subject to numerous external influences, as well as many internal pressures and stressors. These circumstances are never stagnant; the experiences are fleeting and ever-changing.

The interactions that exist involve a complex process that can be impacted by family members as well as anyone else with whom the family interacts during the day. Because there are so many outsiders who may influence the system—extended family, therapists, teachers, friends—the situation can and will alter from moment to moment.

Circumstances that affect the family dynamic vary, but can include: the emotional stability or strength of any family member, the acceptance and adjustment of the individual family members, a shift in power between family members, the introduction of new relationships, and the emotional influences of outsiders on family members. As such, it is essential to consider each family member singularly and the group as a whole. Any change in a single individual or that individual's response to the situation, interaction, or outside influence, can alter the system entirely.

Creating a Family Unit is an Evolutionary Process

When discussing any family, special needs or not, it is not just about two parents who are married with children, but any combination of caretakers and children that distinguish themselves as a family.

In today's world, the definition of family has changed. Beyond the so-called traditional family, there are single-parent families; there are blended families of previously divorced parents and their respective children and stepchildren all living in the same household; there are same-sex parents raising children together; and so on. Regardless of how your family is defined, the inclusion of a child with special needs among other siblings, will present the same set of challenges. What may be of impact, however, are the ways your family chooses to grow together and the role that each family member plays. The relationships that each sibling has with one another, and the relationship that parents have with each child, regardless of whether they are blood relatives or not, will have a considerable influence on the family's stability. In a divorced family, having a child with special needs may require parents to put their differences aside for the sake of the children. Step/half/or part-time siblings need to understand their importance and how best to fit in. Parents must stress how everyone's role and contribution within a family unit is valuable in shaping both individual and family well-being.

The ability to acclimate to and integrate a child with special needs into the family is a very complex process. Some siblings rise to the occasion and are able to adjust well; others may lose interest or may never be able to adapt at all.

Raising a child with special needs and his or her siblings involves an ongoing process of change as family members evolve. Over time, both the parents and the children will go through a series of emotional adjustments that may include feeling depressed, angry, guilty, or all of these emotions simultaneously.

In some instances, the changes that occur are due to the natural progression of development. Just as each child will need new sneakers every year and a child who is in a wheelchair may need refitting every few years, the emotional needs of the children and the family may frequently change. These emotional fluctuations may not be as evident or as easily fixed as purchasing a new pair of shoes, but will become exacerbated if ignored.

New issues will arise with all of the children as they go through various stages and phases. The impact of these changing circumstances will vary as family members adapt or lose their ability to cope.

Some siblings change their acceptance with age. Some may become more accepting and better able to cope as they realize that the situation is long term and unlikely to change. As they become more settled and independent, some siblings may assume more responsibility in the home shared with a child with special needs. Others may find that the long-lasting effect of sharing their life with a child who may not be developing and progressing as much as they are, causes them to feel guilty and as such, they choose to cooperate in order to gain allegiance with their parents. Yet, others become overwhelmed and may choose to act out or distance themselves from the family.

Though there are families that continue to struggle throughout the many years that their children are growing up at home, most families learn to work together and become more cohesive. These families are often more resilient and know they can rely on one another both for emotional and practical support to care for the child with special needs and to receive the care and support that they will need.

Family members usually develop a strong bond due to the frequent crises that arise and the need to work together to resolve them. There is a unique sense of accomplishment and pride shared by family members when these problems are resolved or when goals that seemed so far out of reach are finally attained. In fact, due to the challenges they face and the frequent periods of chaos and ambiguity, the elation that is experienced during the good days may be that much more monumental and become a source of strength for the family.

All About Feelings

As touched upon earlier, there are common experiences and characteristics that all special needs families share. These include feelings of isolation even when there are others around, or simply being misunderstood—as if no one else knows or understands the challenges we face.

You may find that you—or your spouse or children—are reluctant to discuss your feelings with one another because no one wants to burden or stress other family members. You may feel isolated when needing to separate the child with special needs from other people in public to avoid a potentially difficult or embarrassing situation. You and your family members may become frustrated or sad when choosing to stay home in order to avoid having to explain a behavior, outburst, or sudden tantrum. At times, it may be too difficult to dress up and put on a happy face.

Even when attending an event that is focused on or specifically designed for children with special needs, you may feel there really is no one else in the room that shares *your* experience. The diagnoses may be the same, but the behaviors or ways in which the limitations are expressed, may be different. You may often find yourself looking around trying to find the one person who may be feeling as you do.

You may also feel overwhelmed or that your situation is out of control. You try to be the best parent to all of your children, but often feel that you aren't doing enough for any one of them. Then the guilt sets in.

You feel guilty that the time spent doing any one activity with a family member could or should be spent in a different way. You feel guilty that something you might have done has brought this situation on your family. Guilty feelings may even arise when you feel good because you wonder whether someone else in your family might be feeling sad.

There is little point in denying or minimizing these feelings because the reality is that your situation is one you cannot change or control. Just when you pinpoint those aspects of your experience that may be causing the stress, that moment passes and a new crisis arises.

Releasing Appropriate Emotions in Appropriate Ways

In my practice, I observed three types of family adjustment. When faced with a crisis or emotionally charged situation, one group showed tremendous anger, resentment, and sadness. Some family members expressed their emotions more openly than others. In those situations in which the negative emotions were expressed, everyone, including outsiders, was aware of them.

In families in which parents were very angry and negative, the children often felt that it was unsafe to express their emotions. They feared that if they were to convey their negative feelings about their sibling with special needs, their parents might either explode with rage or fall apart emotionally, which, in turn, would impact their parents' ability to be able to continue to care for them. Often the children in these families were high achievers. They worked hard to excel in school and to avoid burdening their parents further. They tried to be compliant and not make too many waves. Sometimes, they appeared to be sad or depressed, but they tried desperately to mask these feelings.

Another group I observed were the families that wore rose-colored glasses. These families worked hard to make everything seem okay—for themselves and to outsiders.

Just as it was difficult to be surrounded by negative emotion, being a member of a family that is always positive, regardless of the circumstances, requires a great deal of emotional energy. You could practically see the glue that was holding these family members' smiles in place. In fact, many of the children in these households walked around on eggshells to maintain a happy façade. They intellectualized their feelings, talking about them rather than feeling them. Everyone was expected to maintain the charade at all times. Parents would report how well adjusted their children were and the children were expected to play that part. In some instances, the performance was only for the outside world. In these families, everyone was struggling at home, but when they were out of the house, they would all put their best face forward. The pressure of holding it together for the sake of others was overwhelming.

In my experience, it was most common to find families in which one parent was extremely emotional and the other overly withdrawn. Similarly, their children were split between those that expressed their emotions and those that did not.

In our home, we were very open about our reactions to our situation and frequently shared both positive and negative feelings with each other and those close to us. We often used humor and laughed together as a family. Our dinner table was like a therapy session, in which anyone could share feelings about anything.

However, on the bad days, our children have seen us cry when we felt overwhelmed and frustrated. Even though we tried our best to keep our interactions private, they sometimes heard us raising our voices, sometimes at each other, because we felt exhausted, angry, and vulnerable by the pressure of our responsibilities. But they came to understand that expressing those feelings was acceptable and encouraged.

Our children have also heard us express a great deal of pride when Jonathan accomplished something new, however small. They have shared our joy, and laughed along with us when we repeated the funny things he said. When he showered us with kisses and hugs, they shared the love and appreciated him, too.

It is essential to let your children know that you are human and have feelings too. Children are more perceptive than we think and, as such, it is not always necessary to minimize the reality of your situation. There are parts of it that are difficult and painful and your children know it. When you can, and in ways they can understand, be honest with your children about your sad or angry feelings but remember to also share the good and positive ones when you experience them. It provides your children with an incredible life lesson—that bad feelings make you stronger and help you to appreciate the good feelings that much more.

Crisis Management and Leadership

In the many years that I worked professionally with families, I learned a lot about the ambiguity of life and how our lives may be overwhelming at times. While there is so much in life that we cannot control, we *can* control our reactions to each new situation.

I worked with many different families, some of whom had a great deal of support yet were barely holding it together, while others were completely on their own and handling the situation with great confidence. Some families adjusted quickly and others never adapted to the situation at all. Some family members felt trapped and others kept going along even though they were unaware of where life would lead them.

I came to recognize that the most essential predictors of a family's ability to work through a crisis were the coping strategies used by family members soon after a life-altering event.

The way in which family members dealt with adversity in the past and their ability to use those tools each time their world was unraveling was a critical aspect in determining that family member's capacity to adapt. In most instances, those who faced previous challenges with strength and courage would proceed with determination. Those who kept their feelings inside did the same when facing a new crisis, but were destined to explode or deteriorate at some point. Those who were functioning marginally before the trauma occurred were most likely to succumb to another trauma and require the most support.

After a critical event, family dynamics were revealed. There was usually a leader, often the mother or father, but at times, a grandparent or friend who would take charge right from the start. That person became the primary communicator for the rest of the family and would try to fix everything for everyone else. That leader would control the emotions of the group. When he or she was feeling confident, everyone else would follow; if that person became doubtful about the situation or the family's ability to cope, the entire family would fall apart.

If you or your spouse are not apt to take a leadership role, perhaps a parent or sibling might be able to provide assistance and support during challenging or transitional times, until you reach a point where you can begin to take the lead. Let that person help you navigate and communicate, especially during the most challenging times.

Children and Responsibility

In most families, children are expected to assume more responsibility as they mature. But in a special needs family, there is a tendency for the siblings to assume—or be delegated—more responsibility for their disabled brother or sister. Having too much responsibility can be detrimental to the siblings' development and their ability to establish their own identities outside of the family.

This is not to say that your children should not occasionally help care for their sibling with special needs, but rather, that you should avoid creating a situation in which they feel obligated to assume that responsibility. Encourage them to interact with their siblings rather than merely care for them. Relationship building is also character building and all the children will benefit.

Whenever possible, seek out someone other than your children to take the responsibility of caring for their sibling. As they get older and more independent, you should try to find outside assistance rather than put the responsibility on the siblings. If the budget allows, hiring babysitters or caregivers can be helpful. If not, recruit trustworthy extended family members, neighbors, or friends.

Wavering Support

A sensitive topic to discuss, but one that special needs families understand, is that we are truly unique, and outside reactions and responses to our circumstances may be different and challenging.

Every child given a heartbreaking diagnosis will evoke great sympathy and compassion. That reaction leads to relatives, friends, and neighbors offering help and support, at least until a recovery is made. But when a child's diagnosis is one that has a lifelong impact—whether autism, cerebral palsy, Down syndrome, muscular dystrophy, etc.—there is no true recovery, so that support inevitably begins to wane and a sense of abandonment sets in for the family.

Further, depending on the child's behavior or level of disability, you may find those you trusted or relied on slowly begin to back off awkwardly or with discomfort. The reasons are diverse and solely an issue with the other person—not you or your family—so you should try to put this in perspective and not take it personally. Regardless, this type of reaction can feel devastating and make it difficult to muster the courage to reach out to anyone when help is needed.

At times like this, rather than feeling bitter, become proactive. Seek out assistance from organizations that support your child's condition or parents/peers in your community in similar circumstances. Find volunteers or college students who welcome the experience of working with your child and family and bring compassion, and extra hands, when you need it.

Using Denial as a Coping Strategy

Elizabeth Kubler-Ross, a Swiss-American psychiatrist, is most noted for her theory about the five stages of grief. These stages begin with *denial* and move to *anger, bargaining*, and *depression* before leading, finally, to *acceptance*. This is applicable to the stages of acceptance experienced by a family with a child with special needs, only the stages might occur simultaneously, especially as stress or crises mount. Denial can be short lived because reality will hit you in the face but, in fact, you may occasionally resort to using denial as a coping mechanism. Though there will be a constant struggle in your efforts to find an explanation for or understanding of your circumstances, eventually you will accept your fate and move on.

Along the way, you will experience anger and depression—this is normal and justifiable. Bargaining may be futile as you realize that you cannot regain control over certain aspects of your—or your family's life—and you may even begin to doubt the presence of a higher power (if you are a person of faith). Eventually, you will learn to temper every stage and emotion you experience with acceptance and rationalization so that you can make it through another day.

Interestingly, denial may become an active rather than passive process. Choosing *not* to accept the circumstances may actually help you and your family to gain the internal resources necessary to handle the challenges you confront.

When a child is born with a disability or is diagnosed with a terminal illness, parents need hope. They need to believe that the possibility of a miracle exists and that things can improve. If parents become hopeless, or don't believe in improvement, they may not give their child the opportunities that will result in further development.

Many believe that parents of a child with special needs must get over their denial in order to deal with their situation. I believe that denial is functional and necessary. It comes in the form of accepting that which you can control and ignoring or minimizing the rest. The concept of "active denial" is especially helpful since no one can predict the future and, in the absence of fact, you can continue to hope.

Your children need you. Denial helps you to propel forward and remain functional so that you can continue to care for your family and, particularly, your child with special needs. Books, magazines, TV shows, and newspapers are filled with stories of parents who refused to accept their child's diagnosis as a hopeless situation, and instead pursued solutions. In denying the statistics, the naysayers, or even the wisdom of professionals, some parents become empowered to create a life for their child—for all their children—that is filled with hope and possibilities. Even the smallest dose of denial may transform a bad day or a pessimistic mindset into one of empowerment.

Learning to "Roll With It"

Almost everyone living today experiences some stress and uncertainty. We live in a disposable society in which if anything breaks, we can repair it, find someone who can fix it, or else replace it. Some people enter a job or even marriage knowing that if it doesn't work out, they can quit and try something new elsewhere. There's the opportunity to press the restart button on just about anything in life.

But what if it is your child who isn't working the way he or she is supposed to? You can't give the child back and you can't get a replacement. When dealing with a special needs family there may be many things that break down all at once and it may be impossible to fix any of them.

There comes a point in the lives of special needs families when the parents and children simply "roll with it." Reaching this juncture may not occur intentionally, but gradually, and you will find that each family member must come to this point in his or her own way and time. This sense of acquiescence helps to alleviate stress, conflict, and fear. The more acclimated you become to your circumstances, the easier it gets. Eventually, this becomes part of your "normal" family dynamic, one that builds strength of character.

Establishing New Expectations

As a parent of a family with children who function at different rates and levels, seemingly happy occasions may become completely overwhelming. For example, while the "back to school" experience is thrilling for most families whose children may be moving up from black and white notebooks to binders or from lunch boxes to a cafeteria program, there will always be the child who does not have the opportunity to move on and, if he or she does, will rarely move as quickly as the others. Similarly, the excitement of completing a school year and graduating from elementary to middle school or middle to high school is another sad reminder of milestones not being reached by one member of your family, now or ever.

The sad feelings you experience may draw you to concerns about your children. Will they feel guilty about their sibling's lack of progress? How will your child with special needs feel as he watches his siblings move on? Graduation day or any other milestone serves to reinforce all of the lost opportunities that may never be recouped.

You will be able to measure your child's progress but the steps taken may be in smaller increments. You may even have to look back in order to see the changes that are made.

Snap family photos with your camera, smartphone, or even in your mind. Take the time to actually look at family photos together so that you will all have the opportunity to reflect on the changes and progress that have occurred.

Raising a special needs family is a juggling act. Your may have to stay home to mind your child while your spouse attends an event with your other children. One child may babysit a sibling with special needs so that you and your spouse can have a relaxing evening out.

There may be occasions when you may have to leave your child with special needs behind during special family moments, when taking trips, or attending events or social activities. You may feel guilty when this happens and your other children may feel guilty about enjoying themselves in their brother or sister's absence. Preparing them in advance by discussing why decisions were made and how everyone may feel about them can go a long way in alleviating guilt or remorse.

Though you may not anticipate the many expectations that are changed or lost, you and your children will learn to create and manage new expectations, and will come to understand how it may be necessary to alter your path to stay on course.

The Desire to Protect

All parents have an innate need to protect their children. When dealing with a young child, you may literally have to help pick up the pieces when a toy tower falls or help alleviate the pressure of a first time at bat during T-Ball. For older children, you may have to smooth over the edges when they have a conflict with a friend or help them overcome the disappointment of a bad grade on a test. Even as your children become adults and leave the nest, you may want to protect them from a mean boss or a bad breakup.

If you are raising your children in a loving and caring environment, it is natural for your children to have the desire to protect one another—especially their sibling with special needs. They may want to protect their sibling from harm or from the way others perceive and treat their sibling. The outside world is filled with people who don't understand and are not sensitive to people with differences. Facing the outside world often leads to feelings of rejection and ostracism. And when you are a member of a special needs family, you know that first hand.

The reality is that you do not have the ability to prevent your children's painful growth experiences or make them disappear. But you can be there to support them and comfort them when they have bad days.

The Benefit of Inclusion

I have often been asked why there were fewer children with special needs when we were growing up, and I have several theories about this. In the past, many children born with obvious disabilities were institutionalized for financial reasons or to protect the siblings from emotional pain.

Others were put up for adoption or kept tucked away at home to avoid the rejection from society.

Fortunately, as more children with special needs are out in the world, we have made a great deal of progress in acceptance and accommodation. There are many more inclusive opportunities available for our children with special needs, and hopefully even more will be available to future generations.

Families should embrace the opportunity to include their child with special needs in the community. As a unit, the family can support each other through these outings so that they may weather the adversities they face.

Inclusion has become a powerful tool that our families share. Encourage your children to feel proud of their sibling and face the world from a position of strength. Encourage your children to know that the outside world will benefit as much from their exposure to your special child as your family experiences from this opportunity every single day.

Show How Much You Enjoy Parenting Each of Your Children

Every empty nester will tell you that children grow up quickly. One day you are changing diapers and the next day you are walking that child down the aisle to be married. One day you are painfully struggling to understand your child's difficult diagnosis and the next day you are bursting with pride when she masters a skill that helps her to be more independent. Time moves quickly, especially in retrospect, so if you don't stop to embrace moments of joy while raising your children, you will likely regret it.

When you experience a special or touching moment with any of your children, share it with the others—let them know what you appreciate about it. Let them know you care about the things that are important to them and that you are enjoying yourself because of the time you share together. Encourage your children to do the same with each other.

Don't fall prey to peer pressure or media messages that suggest there is an ideal parent or an ideal family. Create your "ideal" by embracing and extolling your family's unique dynamic.

Most of all, remember to let your children know they are loved and accepted for exactly who they are, regardless of differences or limitations. Raising children to become competent, independent, strong, and self-assured adults is the ultimate objective for most parents. Though they may not always be easy to deal with, especially during those teenage years, their confidence and determination will take them a long way and you can enjoy their successes knowing that you played an essential role. And know that this role never changes, even after they leave the nest.

Make the most of the time you have with your children. When they are younger, find the time in each day to share an activity that the children enjoy, both one-on-one and together, not just for them, but also for you. As they get older, make sure to reach out to them and connect with them often. If they are away from home, take a minute to call and say hello.

These are the moments you and they will cherish and remember. The more opportunities you have to bond with your children, the more you will enjoy being a parent and your children will enjoy having you as their parent. This will help to remind you and them that in a special needs family, all children are special—and you are, too.

Summary Points
- You are not alone. All special needs families share common emotions and concerns.
- Family life is fluid and family members are interconnected and susceptible to changing circumstances and outside influences.
- Understanding and talking about feelings together as a family builds trust.

- Special needs families need someone—preferably you, as the parent—to lead.
- Brothers and sisters should not be obligated to care for their special needs sibling, but can benefit by engaging with them.
- A child with special needs presents a long-term care situation that requires many levels of support inside and outside the home.
- Being in denial, at times, about a child's condition can often motivate parents to see beyond limitations and maintain optimism.
- Try to put aside your expectations and learn to "roll with" life as it unfolds for you and your children.
- Let each of your children know that they are special and loved in their own way.

Chapter 3: Parental Empowerment and Care

All parents learn on the job. We have little training other than our experience of being parented during our own childhood. We may have a perception that the approaches used by our parents are ideal and we may want to model them; or we may believe that our parents made many mistakes and we chose to take our own path. Our spouse or partner may also have a different concept of parenting based on his or her childhood experience. Over time, you will develop a style of your own, and hopefully it will mesh with your partner's approach.

Being a primary caregiver in a special needs family is different, however. In most instances, your parents did not have a special needs child, and therefore, you do not have a role model to guide you. You are inundated with a myriad of responsibilities that must be dealt with at any given moment, but there are no guidelines as to which situation is the priority. You may have to address the medical, physical, social, emotional, and financial issues of one child who may be completely dependent on you, while balancing the needs of several others who also need and depend on you. You are a decision maker, problem solver, peacekeeper, confidant, mediator, and cheerleader for *all* of your children.

And, if that isn't enough, you also must deal with doctors, teachers, therapists, and the bureaucracy of institutional systems that may place unrealistic demands on your time and patience. You must juggle it all simultaneously and keep all the balls in the air.

There may be times when things seem to be working well and times when nothing seems to work at all. There may be days when you feel good about your ability to handle your responsibilities and other days when all you can see is doom and gloom. Sometimes you won't be able to imagine how you will get through another day.

In a special needs family, parents are thrust into a position of extraordinary responsibility with very little experience or knowledge about what lies ahead. In the best of circumstances, parents wear many hats, but in raising a special needs family, there are even more of them.

When things are not working out to your liking at a particular moment, you should not lose faith; just try something new tomorrow and hope for a better day.

The Worry Factor

Worrying about your family is natural but should not become debilitating. You may worry about the impact that your child with special needs may have on your other children. You may worry about the impact on your children's social status, as well as the impact on your finances. You may worry about the imbalance that will exist in your family when one child achieves new milestones and another does not. You may worry about the disappointment your children will face when they can't or don't achieve the goals they set for themselves. Most of all, you may worry about how you'll get through the day.

These worries may overwhelm you—more so if you feel you are responsible for comforting and reassuring everyone around you. You want to be able to reassure your children that everything will be just fine, even when you're not sure it will be.

If you continue to worry, you risk the chance of becoming consumed by those worries to the point of distraction or detriment to your health. Since you have so much to do, that is not an option. Whenever possible, choose to focus your energy and attention on doing what you *can* do, and then hold on for the ride.

Don't worry about being afraid or ashamed to acknowledge your concerns. It is important and beneficial to identify your worries and fears openly—to yourself, your partner, or a friend. By doing so, sometimes those worries dissipate.

Trusting Your Intuition

Just as there is a great deal of uncertainty about the stress you may encounter from day-to-day, there is also a great deal of fluctuation in the impact that those stresses can have upon you or your family. As such, rely on your instincts to know what is best for your children and for you. This inner sense is what I refer to as "parent intuition."

As parent and caregiver, you know your children better than anyone else. You have spent more time with your children than any teacher, doctor, or professional who may be a part of their life. You can sense when something is working, when it is not, and when to try a different approach. You know what makes your children tick and what gets them ticked off. You know how to get them to cooperate and how to help them move past a problem when they become set in their ways. What's more, your children innately know you are attuned to them and entrust you to look out for them.

As long as you try to do your best for each of your children by focusing on your love and concern for them, there really is nothing you can do that is wrong. This is not to say that you won't make a few mistakes along the way, but as long as your intentions are good, you trust your instincts, and remain focused on each child individually, the outcome should be positive.

You're Only Human

Anger, frustration, and disappointment are emotions everyone experiences and being aware of these feelings is necessary and healthy. Circumstances will trigger these emotions, as will other people. Not just your spouse or children but parents and friends. There are many people—babysitters, teachers, therapists, and even the school secretary—who are or will become an integral part of your life and with whom you will interact or rely on for day-to-day care. With so many people and opinions about, it can often become frustrating and aggravating, especially when you are feeling vulnerable or being subjected to unsolicited advice. On these occasions, keeping your feelings in check may be difficult and you may suddenly lose it.

Don't be too hard on yourself about these occasional outbursts because they will only add to your stress. If your children happen to be the recipients of or witness these outbursts, when you are calmer, you may want to explain how you were feeling at the time, how your reaction may have been inappropriate, and suggest that there might have been a better way to handle the situation. In expressing your mistakes, you will be modeling the importance of identifying our slipups and the need to consider alternative responses. You will be teaching your children the importance of accepting mistakes and moving on.

Sometimes, our so-called spontaneous reactions aren't about the situation at hand, but a build up of many frustrations that result in a loss of control. Try to look at what brought you to that point and try not to be too critical. After all, you are only human.

The same holds true for the myth of believing you must always hold it together. While it is admirable to play the role of "super mom" or "super dad," in actuality, not having to keep it all together for everyone all the time may be the greatest gift that you can give yourself and your family. Realizing that you don't have to succeed in every aspect of your life will help your children accept their own limitations. It will also help you to become a happier person and, in turn, will benefit those you love the most.

Your Children's Needs vs. Your Own Needs

When they are young, your children are dependent on you for everything. You likely want to devote yourself to them fully and unconditionally, even if it means minimizing or giving up your own needs. You may even put your imagination, expectations, wishes, and dreams on hold. You may put yourself on the back burner knowing that in due time, after your children are off to college or out on their own, you will eventually regain some of your freedom, independence, and identity.

But, in the case of raising a child with special needs, that goal of independence for yourself may be difficult to reach, as your child may remain dependent on you well into adulthood.

Early on, it may seem that your child with special needs requires supervision during every waking moment, and some may require supervision even while they are asleep.

Taking care of a child your whole life may seem a daunting responsibility. As such, it becomes critical to balance your own needs with your role as a parent. Don't feel that you must do this all on your own or that you are a bad parent if you reach out for help.

It is likely that your child with special needs will make progress toward becoming more independent. Some may even be able to be left alone for a period of time or you might be able to provide supervision from greater distances. The time will come when they, like your other children, will be able to engage in activities of personal interest on their own and you will be able to engage in yours. It may take a bit longer than you planned, but the time will come when your child with special needs will become so engrossed in a hobby or interest that they may want you to leave them alone.

And, for those who cannot be left on their own, the time will come when you will find other equally qualified people who will be able to care for your child as you do.

Therefore, while you may not be able to achieve all of your dreams, you should be sure to dream often. With a little planning and coordination, you can make time each day to be completely on your own. Though you may not be able to do everything you want for yourself, you should take care of yourself so that you can do everything you want for your family.

Acknowledge and Accept What You Can and Cannot Control

This is perhaps one of the most important messages for parents in general, and is most assuredly the motto by which I have come to live my life. When parenting a child with special needs, there are many things that are out of control, chaotic, and demoralizing. There are many experiences and people who you love that you cannot change, improve, or alter no matter how hard you try.

But you *can* control your reaction to your out-of-control life. Start each day anew, realizing that while you cannot control the feelings and experiences of the people around you, you can control or change the way you *react* to those people and their behaviors. When you feel yourself getting stressed or agitated, take a moment to breath, and realize it is better—and healthier—to let things go.

There may be times that you won't have a clue what to do next or how to fix a problem. There may be many situations that seem unmanageable. At those times, you have three choices: reflect back on the past to what has worked before; try something new; or do nothing and hope that it will pass.

I can't count the number of times that I have used the phrase, "this too shall pass," in reference to a seriously disruptive behavior or a difficult stage that one of our children went through. Reminding myself that time does not stand still, especially in dealing with children, was often the boost I needed to get through another day. When you feel that the situation is completely out of control, know that it will pass or resolve.

New days bring new challenges. The constant change helps you to develop stamina, ingenuity, and resolve. Take comfort in knowing that while the challenges may change over time, you are uniquely qualified to face them.

Tips for Taking Care of Yourself

It's not always about the children. Sometimes, it needs to be about *you*. As the saying goes, "If mama ain't happy then nobody's happy"— and that goes for dad, too. There are many ways to take care of yourself so that you can, in turn, pull from the inner resources you need to manage your unique family. Here are some tips that you can follow:

- **Put yourself first.** At times, it is important to put your own needs first so that you have the strength to take care of your children. If you allow yourself to get burnt out, you will be unable to take care of your family effectively.

- **Reassess your priorities and redefine your goals.** Though you may be a neat freak at heart, reassess the value of having a tidy home versus the value of spending more quality time with each of your children. Or, if you feel compelled to prepare daily nutritious meals for your family, opt for take out one night a week so you can have more time to relax at the dinner table with your children and talk about their day. When you have a quiet moment, take a breath and think about what is truly important to you.

- **Set goals and try to accomplish them one at a time.** Keeping a to-do list may seem overwhelming but it may help you organize your priorities and take note of your accomplishments. At times, you may have to break a goal down into several manageable steps. As each step is achieved, you will feel pride in checking it off the list and in knowing that you are moving closer to the finish line.

- **The value of quality time.** Enjoying just a few moments of calm, alone, with your partner or with a good friend, is invaluable and provides strength for dealing with the many challenges you face. Similarly, spending quality time engaged in a fun activity with your children is rejuvenating and helps you to appreciate them more. Take the time to enjoy those special moments with the people you love.

- **Try to lower your expectations**. Recognize that you don't have to resolve every problem and that your resolution does not always have to be successful. A partial fix may be better than none or it may be good enough to get you through the day.

- **Get enough sleep.** As special needs parents, our "special needs" do include getting proper rest. On days when you can't meet that 7-8 hour norm, the next best remedy is to simply catch a "power nap." Switch off any overnight duties with your spouse or try to make up the time on the weekend, if possible. If anxiety or other stressors interfere with your sleep, try to share your feelings with a spouse or friend during the day or do something relaxing before bedtime. Drink a cup of chamomile tea, indulge in a hot bath, spend 10-minutes in meditation, or anything else that creates calm so you can get the sleep you need.

- **Find time to exercise**. Since you are often on an emotional rollercoaster, exercise is extremely beneficial. Exercise releases endorphins that are natural painkillers and a mood elevator. At the same time, stress releases Cortisol that can cause physical and emotional damage when there is no outlet to release it. Many parents have trouble finding time for exercise and this may contribute to their stress. You may find it helpful to create a weekly schedule that includes time for exercise for you and for your children. Find ways to work out as a family. Taking long walks or hiking are good opportunities for exercise that provide quality time in which you could casually engage with your children.

- **Schedule play dates for your children.** It may take some planning, but when your children are enjoying time at their friends' houses, you could find a sitter to spend time with your child with special needs. During those few hours in which your children are happy and content, you can enjoy having time to yourself.

- **Have a date night with your partner.** When children come along, many couples neglect to take time for themselves and their relationship. This is particularly true when you're parenting a child who needs even more attention. Don't neglect your relationship. Go to a movie or show, have a nice dinner, or take a walk together, but don't talk about the children or the challenges—just focus on each other. Plan an evening out alone together at least once a month to enjoy yourselves and maintain intimacy. These outings don't have to involve expensive activities. Quiet time in a quiet place may be more relaxing and intimate.

- **Keep a journal.** It can be very helpful and therapeutic to write down your thoughts and feelings, whether in a journal, a blog, or just by speaking into a voice recorder. Having an internal conversation will help you to express your feelings and concerns, clarify problems, and suddenly find solutions. Releasing your feelings is healthier than keeping them bottled up inside.

Even if you don't immediately solve your problems, you will feel better getting these feelings off your chest. Once the feelings are expressed, it is easier to consider the solutions or move on.

- **Pursue a hobby.** Hobbies and outside interests are very beneficial. These activities give you the opportunity to take a break and to be creative. When you finish a project, you will feel a sense of accomplishment. You may find other people who share your interests and develop a new support group.

- **Get a helping hand.** If you need help, don't be too shy or too proud to reach out and ask someone to give you a hand. You could rely on a friend or neighbor to do the carpool or take your child out on an errand while you are at an appointment with another child. You can not do it all yourself so having others pitch in when needed will give you a chance to accomplish more.

- **Seek counseling.** Whether you choose to work with a psychologist, therapist, life coach, or trusted religious mentor, outside counseling can help you gain perspective and work through concerns. While therapy is beneficial during important transitions in your life, you may also find that maintaining an ongoing relationship with a professional can help you cope with the many transitions that your *children* will go through over time.

- **Have a "do-over."** If you miss an opportunity to share in an activity with your children or teach an important lesson, that opportunity will inevitably arise again. You may also find that if you try to employ a new rule or disciplinary action with your children and it doesn't work, tuck it away and try again at a later time. It may succeed the next time or, if something is unsuccessful with one child, it may work well with another.

- **Maintain balance.** It is important to establish a balance and not to put too much effort into one thing and lose out on another. Life is not perfect and neither are you so focus on the process rather than on getting the project done to perfection. Work on those things that you can get right and dismiss those things that you can't. Take the time to appreciate your efforts, and be proud that you followed through with your goal.

- **Give gratitude.** For any parent who is overwhelmed emotionally or physically, any act of kindness from a spouse, child, parent, sibling, neighbor, friend or even a helpful stranger, is a relief and a blessing. When you are the recipient of these good deeds, taking the opportunity to say "thank you" will actually make you feel better. Send a card or small gift at holiday times or when you think the time is right. You may want to involve your children in baking cookies or creating small gift baskets for teachers, therapists, and friends who help the family. It will teach them the importance of expressing appreciation.

- **Reciprocate.** Many parents feel guilty or uncomfortable about relying on other people for support. A good way to alleviate this feeling is to give back to family and friends who help you. Offer to host a play date, carpool their children, or extend an invitation to dinner or a barbeque at your home. It is a nice opportunity for the people who are part of your life to meet one another.

- **Have a girls' (or boys') night out.** Spending time with friends is valuable and enjoyable. Whether you plan dinner and a movie, a round of golf, or drinks and conversation, spending time with the people you enjoy will help you to relax and gain balance in your life.

- **Prayer or meditation can be helpful.** Prayer does not have to be a spiritual experience. It could be an opportunity to reflect on your day and the day ahead. Taking time to confirm your accomplishments and asking for the strength to go on, will energize you and give you the ability to do more for others. If nothing else, the brief period of peace and quiet has enormous benefit. Taking a bath or a drive at the end of a long day is a wonderful opportunity for quiet time and meditation.

- **Share your successes**. You've worked hard to keep yourself and your family going. Share your successes and accomplishments with your family and friends. This is not to suggest that you have to brag, but rather, that you recognize your own worth and share it with the important people in your life. When you value yourself, others will value you more. After hearing about your children's day, take a moment to talk about *your* activities and accomplishments. The experience of sharing will help your children to value your contribution in their life and understand another person's perspective.

- **Give yourself a pat on the back.** You deserve praise from yourself. Be cognizant of all of the strengths that you have and all that you have achieved. Take a moment to recognize that you got through another challenging day, and that in the course of that day you have helped each of your children and yourself grow in many ways.

Alleviating Your Guilt and Letting Go

Many parents feel guilty when doing things for themselves or putting their needs first. Try not to succumb to this. You need and deserve a break and should not be apologetic when you take one. Disregard the voices inside your head or even the voices of others who may make you feel guilty about the good things you do to take care of and empower yourself. Similarly, don't allow your feelings to interfere with giving your children the opportunities to exhibit their independence or spread their wings toward new horizons and experiences.

When he was just six-years-old, I succumbed to the pressure of family and therapists who recommended that Jonathan attend a therapeutic summer program for children with special needs. I felt guilty about sending him away, especially since he had limited language skills and might not be able to let us know whether he was unhappy.

Because I was told that it would be beneficial to his development, I did not want to deny him an opportunity for growth simply because I could not let go. His therapist and the camp director convinced me that through the camp experience he would make more progress than he did with weekly therapy sessions. I couldn't argue with the professionals who wanted to help my child, so I finally went along with this plan by rationalizing that I would have more time to spend with my other children during Jonathan's absence. I gave no consideration of the fact that I could benefit from the respite time.

I packed my young son's duffle bag full of clothes and sent him away with a heavy heart. My hopes were very high that he would return speaking in full sentences, conveying his many encounters with nature, and recounting his fabulous interactions with all of his new friends.

On visiting day, we received positive reports from Jonathan's counselors and were told he was adjusting well. As the day drew to a close and it was time to take him back to his counselors, I felt guilty about separating from him for another three weeks. He hadn't really been able to tell me whether or not he was enjoying camp. I knew he was receiving good care but he couldn't tell us, in his own words, whether he wanted to remain. As we approached the main office and met the other children in his bunk, I was quickly overcome by my emotions and began to cry.

The camp director turned to console me and said, "You know there are many professionals who specialize in helping parents and families who have a child with special needs."

I can still recall my response, "But you don't understand. I am the person that people see when they have to deal with these situations."

In my haste to prepare him for camp, I had not taken the time to acknowledge my deep feelings about Jonathan's pending absence or the many feelings I had about his developmental delays.

This was a turning point that helped me to become more self-aware. As a parent, you have to allow yourself the opportunity to let go and then put yourself back together.

Jonathan did make progress that summer and benefitted from being away from the family. I, on the other hand, was still recovering long after the duffle bag was stored back in the attic.

Don't try to minimize or rationalize the guilty feelings and don't allow them to overwhelm you either. Guilt serves no one well. Find time to re-mind yourself that all you can do is your best.

While your feelings are valid, they should empower, not derail you. Rather than feeling guilty about all that a special needs situation can bring on your family, try to remember that children are resilient. They understand more than we think, are adaptable, and handle change much better than we do. When given the opportunity, they make great strides toward independence. Allow your children the time and space to grow without guilt. The end result may be one of great pride and accomplish-ment for everyone.

Summary Points

- Worry is natural, but don't allow it to consume you.
- Trust your intuition—your instincts are usually right.
- Resist the urge to blame or be hard on yourself—you're only human.
- Keep your needs in balance with those of your family.
- Understand and accept that which you can—and cannot—control.
- Make and take time to care for yourself regularly.
- Let go of guilt—it serves no one, especially you.

Chapter 4: Building a Support System

Second to taking care of yourself so you can remain balanced and functional to handle the great responsibility that comes with managing and raising a special needs family, you must strive to build a strong support system. In surrounding yourself with people who can lend a hand or take over when you are burnt out, you can reduce the stress of having to "do it all" and be able to experience more quality interactions with the important people in your life, particularly your children whose emotional and psychological health is dependent on getting the best out of you. Most of all, you will benefit from the tremendous emotional support that all of these people provide.

Creating a Parental Team

If you are married, you and your spouse will have to take the time to critically evaluate your strengths and the contributions that you can each make to the situation. For example, the parent who is more organized or detail-oriented can be in charge of all of the scheduling of the children's therapy appointments and afterschool activities. This skill is extremely valuable when dealing with the numerous intricacies of the medical treatments that include medications and therapies or the details involved in filing documents to get appropriate services. The partner who is the better communicator can take the lead in dealing with the many people who are involved in your children's lives and facilitate communication with teachers, therapists, attorneys etc. One parent may be better at getting your children settled at night while the other may be better at getting the house back in order so that the family can start another day.

It may be beneficial to make a list of your respective strengths and weaknesses and then discuss and determine the roles you will each assume. This is not to say that one person will be responsible for those aspects of your family life exclusively, but rather that the person who is best at the task will assume the primary responsibility knowing that the other partner will be there for back-up.

These roles can evolve, as your children get older. Just as you may have a performance evaluation at any job, you will want to communicate your likes and dislikes with your partner and discuss ways that you could improve your performance, perhaps with more support from them. For example, a parent who is uncomfortable handling a young infant or toddler may be an incredible basketball coach or confidant to an adolescent. One parent may prefer staying home playing board games and the other may enjoy bike riding. Because you are dealing with children at different developmental levels and your children may have different strengths and weaknesses, you can determine the various tasks to each undertake, and the roles you will play towards caring for and bringing out the best in each of your children.

It is possible that one of you may have to do more of the "heavy lifting." If one parent works outside of the home and the other is home full-time, there may be an understanding that the parent who is at home with the children is primarily responsible for the day-to-day activities in the home. The parent working outside the home should be cognizant of the tremendous burden of handling therapy appointments, afterschool practices, homework, meals, and bath time, simultaneously for several different children and take more of the lead responsibility on the weekend.

If you feel that your partner is not being supportive enough, take the time to discuss your feelings rather than push them aside. You may come to the realization that you are both working outside your comfort zone or that you both feel burdened by the added responsibility. Together, you may decide that you need additional support from someone who has the skills to help fill in the gaps.

At times, you may disagree about parenting styles, and this requires thorough discussion to determine whether one parent's approach is better than another in dealing with a specific child's needs. Help each other discover the parenting strengths that you have and support each other's efforts to interact with each child individually.

If you find that your partner is not on board, start the conversation by finding common ground and seeking a mutual understanding that you are working together to raise your children in a loving environment. If you can agree on that, then the discussion should focus on the ways that you can each contribute to that goal. Try to avoid statements that reflect your animosity or feelings of neglect, and focus instead on each partner's contributions and ways that through cooperation the team efforts can grow.

If your conflicts require more specific attention, it would be beneficial to pursue couples or family counseling from a trained professional who can guide you through a discussion about dividing responsibilities and being supportive of each other's efforts.

It does not matter what the family structure is—husband/wife, single parent with family members and friends that help, or even a divorced couple that is living apart—there must be communication, smart planning, and shared decision-making so that everyone can work together for the benefit of the children. There are many different scenarios and options, but regardless of your family's composition, the key is to set up a supportive system.

Ultimately, if you love and care about your children, you will realize that your goals are the same—to foster the well-being of everyone in your family.

Maintaining the Balance

There are many aspects of communication, support, and compromise that must be established so that you and your partner find a balance in your responsibilities and with each other.

- **Share the burden—and your feelings—with your partner.** If and when there is a problem, identify it, analyze it, and then try to solve it. Avoid becoming a silent sufferer that takes on the responsibilities and then feels burdened by them. Communicate your feelings without accusation and in a manner that commends your partner's efforts and accomplishments. Work with your partner and encourage one another to take on a part of the responsibility to find a solution. Be proud when you solve a problem together and use the experience to reinforce your bond and to build your relationship to be able to solve future challenges.

- **Live every day with purpose and joy.** Recognize that each day brings new opportunities to share good times and appreciate the relationship you share with your partner. Take the time each day to talk about the good experiences that you share and not just the problems.

- **Pat yourself—and your partner—on the back.** Give yourself—and your partner—an "A" when you do something right. It is tremendously reinforcing to give and to receive recognition for accomplishments. As parents, we try our best to let our children know when we are proud of them; as partners, we must do the same. Parents should be supportive of each person's contribution and reinforce this message to your children so that they can appreciate your efforts and not take either of you for granted.

Take the time to express, or even better, to show your love and appreciation.

- **Negotiate the differences**. You and your partner will not always be able to agree on how to deal with a problem but you can still find a solution together. That may mean that one of you will have to compromise, but there will be other opportunities to handle things the other way the next time around.

- **Make time for yourselves as a couple**. This is valuable guidance for any couple but is especially important for those who are raising a child with special needs, since your relationship is the foundation on which everything else is built. Spend time together every day, even if it is just a five-minute telephone call to tell your partner you are thinking about them. Take the time to engage in an activity you both enjoy, whether going to the coffee shop or taking a walk, at least once a week. Plan an extended period of time together—a week's vacation or a few long weekends away—each year. During those times together, however brief, take the time to focus on your relationship and nothing else, knowing that everything else will wait for you. The strength you gain from the bond you share with your partner will help sustain you through the many challenges you will face.

- **Recognize when it is necessary to seek outside counseling**. If you and your partner are unable to find ways to work in a unified manner, wind up fighting, or have difficulty coping, it may be time to seek outside support from a trained professional. It is unhealthy and detrimental to allow conflicts and resentments to escalate and explode. This is all new to you and there are many situations that you are not equipped to resolve on your own. Admitting when you need the help is the first step to resolution.

For Divorced or Single Parents

There are many parents who are not living together due to divorce or separation, as well as those who are single parents by choice. These circumstances bring distinctive challenges to an already complex situation, but there are ways to make things more workable.

If you are divorced, I would strongly encourage you to work together with your ex as a team. As difficult or even impossible as that may sound, the reality is that children whose parents work together in raising them tend to have greater self-esteem and fewer behavioral issues. They benefit from knowing and seeing first hand that regardless of their conflicts and dissimilarities, their parents put those differences aside to work cooperatively and meet everyone's needs, including those of the sibling with special needs.

If there is a great deal of conflict between you and your ex, it is often beneficial to seek professional help so that you can better negotiate and work out your differences. You may even consider sharing the cost of this professional help equally, as the first sign of your commitment to work together for the sake of your children.

In raising your children, apart or together, it is critical to establish common rules and goals for your children to follow. Though the houses may look very different, children need to understand that the expectations and consequences will be the same regardless of which parent is in charge at any given moment. This is especially important for the child with special needs who may have a particular communication or behavior system in place, or special dietary restrictions, that must be followed in all situations. Supporting one another through the parenting process will help the children to feel more secure and will minimize the opportunities for the children to act out.

Single parents have a unique situation and may depend even more on outside help from their parents, siblings, friends, or other moms or dads in a similar situation. While you do have the luxury of being in charge and not having to negotiate with a partner regarding differences of opinion about care and intervention, you may be more likely to feel burdened and overwhelmed.

Seeking the support of the many organizations and support groups that are available for the families of children with special needs may prove invaluable. Take advantage of the many programs that these organizations offer and try to develop relationships with other parents and their children—these friendships can be of benefit to your children as well. One parent could care for the children with special needs while another parent goes out to the movies with the other children. If your children share common interests, you may be able to plan a weekly dinner or a weekend trip together.

Creating a Support Team

If you are fortunate to have extended family nearby, reach out and recruit them as part of your support team. Having your parents, grandparents, siblings, cousins, and close friends available, will help you to maintain your emotional health.

If willing, these individuals can provide invaluable assistance. They can spend special time with each of your children and share their talents with them. They can take your children to appointments and be there for you so that you don't feel you are on your own.

Take the time to evaluate your situation to determine the type of help you may need and then delegate those responsibilities to the appropriate member of your team. Ask your team members to clarify the activities they feel most comfortable doing and ask your children which activities they enjoy sharing with the different members of your team.

Doctors, teachers, therapists, home health aides, tutors, clergy members, and coaches can all become members of your support system. Many of them may know other families with children with special needs and they may be able to provide information about the resources and programs that are available in your community. If you are comfortable sharing your circumstances with them, these people may have a great deal of wisdom based on their years of experience. Many of these people are just creative by nature, and may be able to help you think outside the box.

As previously mentioned, your greatest source of support and reinforcement will likely come from other special needs families. You may find that you have a great deal to share with one another. You may be able to work out a system in which one family assumes the responsibility of covering childcare responsibilities while the parents of the other family share some alone time. You may want to plan family outings or even vacations together for camaraderie. Together, the families could share the expenses incurred when traveling with and accommodating for children who have special needs, such as getting a babysitter or an aide. Your other children will value spending time with children their age who share their experiences.

As you extend your circle to include the many other people who care about you and your children, you will cease to feel alone and become less overwhelmed by many of the challenges you face.

Teach Your Children the Skills to Join the Team

Just as you have to teach them to crawl before they can learn to walk and to dribble a ball before they can shoot, it is important to teach your children the skills to becoming a sibling of a child with special needs. As previously mentioned, some children are born with the ability to care for other people and are a bit more compassionate. But regardless of their ability to nurture or their need to learn the skills, these children will be caring for their siblings for the rest of their lives. As such, it is essential to gradually reinforce each child for their efforts to give to and take care of their siblings who may not be able to take care of themselves.

Starting at a young age, your children will have the opportunity to observe many adults caring for their sibling and they will try to model these behaviors. As they observe their parents, extended family members, and the many therapists and specialists interacting with their sibling, they will perceive this as "grown up" behavior and want to try to do the same. Every effort to care for and protect their sibling, however small, should be identified and reinforced.

A very young child could retrieve wipes or get their sibling's favorite toys so that they can play together. Even at a young age, your child could act as a teacher or role model for their siblings, helping them make a sandwich or pour a cup a of juice. As they get older, siblings should be encouraged to help out in ways that are simple yet engaging. Just as the adults in your support team should be encouraged to share their strengths and interests with the child with special needs, a sibling should be encouraged to share their interests and interact in a meaningful way.

Though adults perceive many activities to be chores, children often enjoy cooking, helping to care for a baby or grocery shopping, and may be eager to help in the care of their sibling with special needs. Start with simple tasks like putting away toys, pushing a wheelchair or "babysitting" while the two children watch a video together so that you can take a quick shower. Help your children identify age-appropriate activities they can share. Try to balance this responsibility with special privileges that your children will value, such as, an extra hour of TV, video game time, or spending time alone with you at a favorite restaurant.

Your primary goal should be to create positive interactions between your children and to encourage them to feel good about their contribution to the family support team. Through the interaction and your reinforcement of it, your children will feel positively about the many ways that they are able to enhance their special sibling's life.

Managing Your Support Team

Once you have established your support team, which includes your partner or any other adults who may be helping you care for your children, you can take a team approach when dealing with any problems you encounter. Through this process, you gain a great deal of insight about the situation and learn more about yourself. You can reflect on the circumstances that caused you or your child to become frazzled and ways that you might avoid those pitfalls in the future.

Reaching out for help involves asking other people for advice but may at times require asking other people to step in and take over. Because of all of the responsibility that you carry, it is essential to work with the members of your support team and take turns being in charge. It is comforting to know that when you are under the weather, having a bad day, or just feeling exhausted or overwhelmed, someone else will be there to pick up the slack.

You could share the responsibility of addressing the day-to-day circumstances you face, or dealing with the many individuals who are involved in your children's lives. You could discuss the decisions that are as simple as what to serve for dinner and as life altering as where your child with special needs will attend school.

There may be times that you feel like giving up, but when you have a support team in place, there's always someone to call upon during those times when you need a break.

As a parent who is primarily responsible for other people, not always having to be in charge requires a certain degree of confidence and self-recognition. You have to be aware of your personal strengths and be able to identify when someone else can do a better job as the caregiver temporarily. Delegating a team member to take the lead for a time will not alter your role within the family and you will be able to resume your responsibilities when you are ready.

Parents, and other individuals who are involved in providing care for the children in the family, should work together in a unified manner. Even when the person pitching in has a different style or approach, if you can clearly communicate what you need help with and a schedule of when to get things done, you can more easily relinquish control. Your team is there to alleviate stress, not create more of it.

Your Emergency Contact List

The support team will be critical players, especially in emergency situations.

Create an emergency contact list and share it with everyone on that list as well as keeping it posted in a visible place at home. In addition to family members who live nearby, your emergency contact list should include babysitters and neighbors that are willing and able to pick your sick child up at school and keep them safely in their house until you can get home. Those same people can be called on when you are stuck at a doctor's appointment with one child and another child is getting off the bus at your house.

Establishing House Rules for Your Support Team

To an outsider, life in a special needs family may seem as busy and colorful as a three-ring circus with different activities occurring all at once. And parents are the ringleaders who keep everything and everyone moving. There may be times in which parents, a grandparent or babysitter, and an in-home therapist, are in the home simultaneously and each has a specific role or a designated child in their care. This flurry of people and their comings and goings, can become confusing for all your children—not just young ones—and requires a set of rules that apply to those situations.

Communication is critical among caregivers and between the caregivers and the children. Ideally, your children should understand that they could have more than one caregiver and should be able to smoothly transition between them. Therefore, it is essential to establish "house rules" and to respect one another's authority.

If you fail to make it clear to your children that there may be several caregivers and that each has the authority when they are in charge, your children may try to play one caregiver against the other to get their own way. Your children should understand that the caregivers work together as a team and that any one—or all of you—may be in charge at any given time and the same rules apply.

It is important to consider not only the personalities of the individual children but also the personalities of each of the caregivers in determining how to best maintain the balance in your family.

Personal chemistry is a factor when examining these relationships. An easy-going child may require the structure of a more rigid caregiver while the demanding and uncompromising child may benefit from a more accommodating caregiver. The caregivers who help your family should be able to determine what each child requires and to provide that interaction as consistently as possible.

When you must rely on caregivers—whether family members, friends, or those you employ—the family structure will remain intact if the rules are already in place. Children feel more secure knowing that things will always remain the same whether you are there or not. You likely have rules that you set for your children, so in your absence, caregivers should adhere to those rules. Make sure that they know and understand them. Make a list of these rules—as well as the responsibilities each of your children have in the household—and post it on the refrigerator or another place of prominence. If there are unique circumstances that impact a daily routine, those details should be discussed with your team in detail— and in advance—to avoid confusion or misunderstanding. You may want to post a family calendar that includes each child's daily activities and the designated caregiver to avoid confusion amongst the caregivers and help orient your children to the plan when they become confused.

There are rules you have about handling childcare that should also be expressed. For example, if you have strong feelings about the types of foods that a child eats or the preferred language that should be used in dealing with the child with special needs, all members of your support team should be apprised of these rules and respect and support that system when in your home. If caregivers have ideas or ways of doing things that are comfortable to them, they should have the opportunity to discuss this with you, too. In fact, scheduling a meeting with everyone together, either every month or every other month, will give your team a chance to discuss how things are working and become a forum to share ideas and get feedback about how children are behaving or managing when you are not around.

Connecting with the Special Needs Community

As mentioned previously, you may benefit from participating in either formal or informal support groups with other parents who have children with special needs. Because of the unique experiences they share and the challenges they face on a daily basis, the parents of a special needs family are among the most resilient and creative people you will meet. These individuals demonstrate strength and tenacity and, despite the ever-changing challenges, keep coming back for more. They display a great deal of character and this is especially remarkable considering that not one of them was prepared for the circumstances in which they found themselves.

When we identify a kindred spirit, we eagerly offer and ask for suggestions and advice. We innately know how desperate and lonely it feels when trying to cope with or resolve our issues and are eager to spare others from having that same feeling or experience. Caregiving becomes not just something we do for our children, but what we do for one another.

Over the years, I have participated in athletic leagues for children with special needs, established a knitting circle, and played Mah Jongg with the mothers of other children with special needs. While sharing common interests and enjoying activities together, we have also come up with clever solutions for raising our unique families.

We shared information and offered recommendations regarding therapists, camp programs, lawyers, dentists, and specialists to accommodate a child with special needs. We have even developed support programs for the siblings.

We soon came to recognize that we are the best problem solvers out there.

Whenever possible, find ways to seek out and connect with other special needs families. Through these connections you will find understanding, empathy, support, and not surprisingly, unconditional love.

Other Circles of Influence

In the many years that I worked as a psychologist, I received—and employed—excellent advice and wisdom from my colleagues. We would often share information, especially about troubling situations, and used each other as a sounding board to discuss challenges or brainstorm solutions.

This approach became an asset when I began to navigate my way through the system as a parent and may be beneficial in dealing with your children. By sharing your frustrations and talking through your ideas about the issues that you are experiencing in your home, with your spouse, family, and friends, you will receive a great deal of support and many good suggestions.

Seek out and surround yourself with a network of people who share similar problems or care about yours. This seems like simple advice, but in reality, it is not always easy to find caring people who are willing to put aside their own problems in life and focus on yours.

With a large social circle that includes family, friends, coworkers, and even a few kind strangers, you will find that everyone has something valuable to contribute. Granted, some of that advice and guidance may be baseless, or not be appropriate for the personality or developmental level of your child or children. But, on the other hand, any well-meaning advice and guidance can help you to feel productive in a situation that may at times feel hopeless. It may provide a direction or something that you can try when you are feeling helpless. You will also feel supported and comforted in knowing that there are people in your world that care.

Accepting Help When Offered

Some people are givers and others prefer to receive. In my opinion, it isn't bad to be one or the other; it is merely important to know who you are.

One thing that I have discovered is that I don't like to be on the receiving end of a relationship. It is comforting for me to be able to help others. It actually gives me strength.

When you are a giver, it may be difficult to accept help or reach out to others when you need it. My suggestion here is to just say, "Yes!"

This may be one of the most difficult adjustments for you. You may avoid asking for help because you feel that if you do, others may perceive you as a weak parent or minimize your problems. It may be complicated to explain what you need in a way that someone else understands.

As parents, many of us tend to put the needs of our children ahead of our own and often feel guilty when we ask someone else—even our own children—to do something for us.

For those who are natural givers, this will make receiving help a little easier.

In accepting help from others, you will feel less overwhelmed. By accepting support, you will retain, rather than use, your resources and be able to direct your efforts and your energy in more meaningful ways. By accepting support, you will be able to support others and feel good about your ability to help them.

If someone offers to carpool, grocery shop, or run an errand, don't interpret this to mean that they perceive you are incapable but rather that you deserve support or a break. Spend the time taking a break or working towards another task. Anything that you can do to lighten your load is acceptable and beneficial. It will free you to engage in more fulfilling activities, including spending quality time with your children and spouse.

Summary Points

- Developing a support team of family, friends, neighbors, and professionals provides backup, encouragement, and assistance when needed.
- Support starts at home between parents, partners, or those you choose to help in caring for your children, so explore ways to create a parenting team.
- You and your spouse/partner should communicate about the roles you will each play as parents and partners and support and encourage each other's efforts.
- When appropriate, your children can become part of your team.
- Your support team will thrive better when one person acts as "team leader." If you are not comfortable in this role, delegate that role to another team member.
- Make sure you create an Emergency Contact list and share that list with the people that will be caring for your children.
- All team members should abide by "house rules" that you set.
- Seek support from and share ideas with other special needs families.
- Ask for and be willing to accept help from others when needed.

Chapter 5: A Blueprint for Successful Family Management

Just as a large corporation must establish a business plan, you should create a family business plan that establishes the goals and priorities for your family. How do you begin?

Understanding Your Parenting Style

Most adults develop and hone their parenting skills on the job. We often use a trial and error method to find the system that works best with each child. We often rely on our instincts or employ the tactics our parents used when raising us. Some of us intentionally parent our children in a style that is different from those of our parents. How we were raised—coupled with our unique personalities and values—will determine our style.

There are many different parenting styles and benefits to each approach. In the 1960s, clinical psychologist, Diana Baumrind, identified several different approaches to parenting. Her initial research has been replicated and applied to many other areas, including cultural differences and the impact on romantic relationships. While these categories have never been directly applied to the special needs family, they can be helpful in understanding and identifying your—and your partner's—parenting style and to see how these styles can be helpful or problematic.

Authoritarian Parenting

In this approach, parents often believe that it is important to raise their children with strict rules and guidelines. As long as the children are under their roof or receiving their financial support, the parents are in charge and will make the decisions for their children. While this approach is beneficial, especially for those children who may be impulsive or have difficulty making good choices, this method of parenting could in fact impede children from learning to take responsibility for their own actions.

It is also not practical for parents to apply too many rules for a child with special needs since it may prohibit the child from gaining a sense of independence. Likewise, the siblings of this child may be expected to be more independent because the parents may be overly involved in caring for the child with special needs. As such, this strict approach may not be ideal in a special needs household.

Permissive Parenting

Permissive parents avoid disciplining their children altogether and try to relate to them as friends. These parents are nurturing and communicative, often providing a great deal of positive feedback without being confrontational. Some may consider these parents to be indulgent but this approach works well with children who are self-critical and fearful of taking risks.

Within a special needs family, parents may tend to be over-indulgent to minimize their feelings of guilt associated with the challenges their children face because of their disabilities or as the siblings of a child with special needs. They may feel that they must compensate for the ostracism and bullying their children face outside their home. If this is the style most comfortable for you or your partner, try to avoid becoming overly indulgent as your children might have difficulty accepting responsibility and managing the discipline that is required in the real world.

Authoritative Parenting

This approach is a compromise between the two previous styles of parenting and provides a middle ground between giving your children too much freedom and being too strict. You can be nurturing and responsive to your children while maintaining expectations and setting limits. In this approach, children are often given choices that are acceptable options for the parents. For example, a parent might give the child the opportunity to select one activity when two choices are provided.

This approach often works best in a home with a child with special needs because it helps all children learn to take responsibility for the choices they make and to deal with the consequences of their actions. The child with special needs and the siblings should be encouraged to make good decisions and take responsibility for the decisions that are made. The process should begin when the children are young and the decisions are small so that by the time the child reaches adolescence they are able to consider the pros and cons and recognize that good decisions yield a positive outcome while bad decisions may lead to negative consequences. It may take time to teach your children to make good decisions, especially with regard to following rules, acting appropriately and even choosing the right friends, but it is necessary and important for all children, including the child with special needs.

Instinctive Parenting

It is ideal to parent each child in a manner that works best for that child. At times, this may require setting more limits with certain children and providing less structure for others. In a family with a child with special needs, making these shifts from child to child may seem impossible but it can be accomplished if you go with your gut. Instinctive parenting involves a great deal of forethought, planning, and flexibility. You will face more challenges than other parents and therefore, it is helpful to take the time to find the best approach to parent each child and use that method as consistently as possible. Use your parenting instincts and follow your best judgment but be prepared to self-correct when the system is not working.

Reconciling Parenting Styles

As parents, you should work together cooperatively to develop the family plan. Discuss those aspects of raising your family that are most important to each of you. If you share similar beliefs about raising confident and competent children, then you should be able to work out the details in order to achieve that goal.

However, if you discover that your parenting styles clash, you will want to work towards finding a way to reconcile those differences so that you can be united in the way you create and implement your plan. Your family needs you to be on the same page and to be consistent.

Admittedly, this is not easy to accomplish. My husband and I had very different personalities and different parenting styles. His parents were Holocaust survivors and survived unimaginable atrocities during their adolescence and early adult lives. But they were survivors and in turn, became dedicated parents. They believed in a direct approach to parenting their children and took great pride in their children's accomplishments. As he became a parent, my husband believed in having clear expectations and rules for our children. He frequently commented that as long as he is a parent (a responsibility he does not take lightly and believes continues for adult children) he would help direct their behavior and provide input on their decisions.

On the other hand, I was raised in an authoritative environment. My mother was a schoolteacher and guidance counselor and my father was a Rabbi and a lawyer. Their careers involved a great deal of negotiation and they brought those same practices into their parenting. In addition to their dual careers, both of my parents were very active community leaders. There were frequent discussions in our home about people's behavior and their life decisions, both good and bad. Though I knew my parents had very specific expectations, rules, and values that were clearly conveyed, there was much compromise in our home. Because of this environment, when I became a parent, I had a more laid back approach than my husband.

Though there were times that our respective styles created conflict, we were able to divide the responsibilities of parenting our children, even taking turns for the responsibility of one child or another based on the specific situation. We were able to play "good cop/bad cop" on many occasions and help our children see both sides of a situation. We were cognizant of the importance of communicating with one another to avoid having the children create conflict between us.

There were times when our discussion became loud and heated, but ultimately we were able to see each other's perspective and work out a compromise that was in the best interest of each child and our family. Even now, as adults, our children have different relationships with each of us, and that works well for each of them.

In the end, we worked together to devise and implement the appropriate parenting system for each child. Though we may have used different approaches, we agreed on the overall family plan: to be respectful of one another and to raise respectful, kind, and giving people who feel loved and secure. Our blueprint may have been revised over time but the overall structure that we built within our home was maintained consistently throughout and continues today.

With regard to raising our son with special needs, I maintained the primary responsibility, but we shared certain aspects of his care. That was due in part to my professional training and familiarity with the complex special needs system, but the other part was due to my parenting style, which was better suited to deal with our son's behavior. I knew that I could rely on my husband for support and guidance, and he trusted my knowledge and judgment in making the decisions that would be best for our son.

Although I was far more responsible for our son's care during the week, my husband acknowledged my responsibilities by taking on more of those tasks on the weekend. Similarly, since I was chief, cook, and bottle washer all week, on weekends, my husband became the designated parent and chaperone for birthday parties and sports events. He took on this role by choice, because he felt that he was missing out on these special experiences with our children due to his busy work schedule. Our lives were complex inside and outside the home, but the desire to make things work for our family was a driving force for overcoming our challenges.

The Art of Compromise

Regardless of the situation or the particular issue that may arise, learning to compromise is key. Compromise does not mean giving up that which is important to you, but rather, to reprioritize and recognize that in a given situation some things may be more important to you than others.

Compromise is essential in your relationship with your team members, whether a spouse or a supportive relative. And preserving your relationship with each of these important people is often far more important than getting your way.

Compromise also means accepting your differences and encouraging each other to "do your own thing." Relying on one another is essential so that all your children get the best that each of you has to offer. It is also critical to share the responsibility and give as much as you get.

It is helpful to take turns being in charge so that neither of you becomes burdened or overwhelmed. Compromise in parenting may also require you to relax your standards. The job may not be done your way but that does not make it wrong. The focus should be on what is best for your family and not just for you. You may have to give up something now so that in the future you are able to get something else that is important to you. By making compromises on the small, everyday things, you will feel that there is someone there that has your back when the going gets rough.

Resolving Your Planning Conflicts

As a couple, if you are experiencing a conflict or have trouble coming up with tactics that are mutually acceptable, the discussions should take place behind closed doors, away from the children. It is important to take time together to air your differences and consider the other person's perspective, but do so privately, otherwise it minimizes the effect of presenting the choices as a united front and the children might try to play one of you against the other. If the children know there is conflict or an unwilling parent, they will try to create conflict between you when they have your ear. Try to be wary of those situations in which your children are trying to get you on their side. In most instances, this may be an indication that your children feel they can sway you to go up to battle on their behalf against a parent who may feel strongly against their position. Consider and help your child to accept a compromise.

Once you are ready to present the choices, try to convey a message that you are unified. When you "play nicely" and work well with other people, your children will do the same. Parents who undermine each other do themselves and their children a disservice. Rules, discipline, tasks, and schedules lose their structure and all children—particularly those with challenges—thrive best when there is consistency.

The best way to get through planning disagreements is to take the focus off your differences and onto those areas on which you agree. Think broadly first. Start by listing those concepts or values that you share, that may also be applicable to any family, such as:

- Supporting and respecting one another
- Providing your children with emotional security
- Helping each family member to achieve their personal best
- Imparting the values that are necessary to survive in society
- Establishing a safe environment in which all family members feel that they are cared for and loved

Next, think about and discuss specific rules that you both believe are important to follow. These might include:

- Speaking respectfully even when there are disagreements
- Keeping an open mind to each other's opinions
- Modeling appropriate behavior for your children
- Supporting one another especially during stressful times

Through finding and focusing on common ground, rather than on the differences, you will be able to work together and communicate better, even when you disagree.

Goal Setting

Once you have determined and addressed more general and values-based objectives of your overall family blueprint, you can move into determining and setting specific goals. Setting goals is important because it helps to keep the family on task and to feel good about each accomplishment. Through a goal-setting approach you are able to determine what needs to get done and to figure out who is best equipped to complete the task.

Setting specific goals for your children helps to define your expectations for them and helps you to recognize when they need outside help to complete a task. For example, if one of your goals is helping each child to be successful in school but one child has difficulty with math, you may have to find a tutor to supplement the instruction. If your goal is to help each of your children develop the skills to communicate their needs, you may have to find a behaviorist or speech therapist to help your child with special needs communicate theirs. Identifying the objective and then determining the steps to complete the task will help everyone meet those objectives more successfully.

In my home, I set goals for each family member to achieve each day, each week, and each month. I had a clear plan for each child that included his or her school, interpersonal, and family goals. As each goal was accomplished, I would check it off and feel better about our situation. It helped me to feel that I was making progress especially when dealing with smaller achievements in raising a child with developmental delay. Setting smaller goals that are attainable helps you feel productive and somewhat in control.

Goals are both short-term and long-term. Short-term goals can be as simple as getting everyone to school, appointments, and practices on time. While this may seem very basic, it can be a huge undertaking and an even greater accomplishment when you have one child at school, another at a therapy session and a third at an afterschool activity simultaneously. Other short-term goals could be creating simple tasks that each child can undertake according to age and responsibility level, like putting away toys, setting and clearing the dinner table, or completing homework assignments. These are the daily routine tasks that once followed regularly keep family life organized and on point.

Your long-term goals can be more far-reaching and may include helping each child achieve academic success within their limits, building self-esteem, fostering growth and independence, instilling family values, and encouraging strong, respectful, and lasting relationships among your children.

In considering your short- and long-term goals, you should discuss how to allocate your time and attention. Family time together is important, but should be balanced with the one-on-one time you will want to spend with the children, both together and individually, and that they will spend with one another. The time you have available to spend with each child daily, including the child with special needs, is probably limited so you will want to strive to make the most of these interactions.

Setting Individual and Family Goals

In setting goals for the individual family members and the family as a whole, it is important to be specific and realistic. Though there may be some overlap in goals, it is important to delineate the goals that apply to each family member, since your expectations for each child may be different or the goals may be achieved at different rates. When goals are achieved simultaneously it will give you the opportunity to check them off each family members' list and give yourself a big check for helping them to get it done.

Spell out the parameters of each goal. What are the criteria for achieving the goal and how will you know when it has been achieved?

For example, you may want to help your children organize their school supplies so that everyone is responsible for their own items. Set up a system with a color-coded basket or locker for each child. You could have a similar color-coded folder that is used for each child's important notices and permission slips.

You may find that a child with special needs requires more frequent reminders or reinforcement of the smaller steps in order to put the larger goal together. As the children walk through the door a single reminder of "everything goes in your locker; notes in the folder" may work for one child, while another child may require a reminder for the first task followed by reinforcement and then a reminder about the second task. As each child becomes familiar with the system, it will become routine rather than a task. One child may accomplish the goal once they no longer require a reminder while for another child you may set a criteria that your child only requires a reminder three times a week rather than daily. You may find that one child will remind another by carrying out the activity day after day, and your role may diminish over time.

Your goals should be measureable, whether they are short-term or long-term. A short-term goal might be that your children remember to complete a household responsibility every day for a week. A long-term goal could be that your children remember to complete their weekly responsibilities for a month. Be sure to set individual criteria for each child so that one child's noncompliance or inaction will not impact another child's accomplishments. By applying measureable criteria, you and your children will be able to gauge their individual progress and feel proud of their accomplishments.

Make sure that the goals you set are achievable, and when you determine that they may not be within your child's ability be sure to revise the goals to be more manageable. You may find that certain goals have to be abandoned for a time and that during that period your child must learn other skills that are precursors to the larger goal.

Be sure to set individual goals that are realistic for each child but keep the needs of the entire family in mind when setting the goals. For example, it may not be realistic to expect a younger child to be fed, bathed and tucked into bed by six at night if you have afterschool or therapy appointments with another child that are scheduled at five-thirty. You may have to fit a nap into your younger child's schedule so that you have the time to get each child's needs met without feeling stressed or overwhelmed. If you are working on helping your child with special needs to be more responsible for his personal items, encourage all family members to put their shoes in the front closet when they get home, so that the child can follow this example. In fact, each family member will benefit from the family working together in this manner in order to reinforce personal responsibility. If the family does not work together, it may become confusing for the child who is expected to put their clothes in the hamper when everyone else leaves their clothes on the floor.

Each short and long-term goal should have a timeframe and you should review these goals frequently to determine whether they remain relevant. Since special needs families often face situations that seem to be insurmountable, the opportunity to achieve both individually and as a family will give your family a sense of accomplishment, as each family member is successful.

Implementing Your Plan

Creating and implementing your family plan may seem like a daunting task but you are likely to become engaged with the process.

Start by establishing a clear definition of roles within the home that delineates the responsibilities of each family member. Help your children to recognize that the more they contribute to the process the greater the possibility of family success.

Young children could contribute through cooperative behavior and taking care of simple tasks that they complete independently. Older children can contribute with specific tasks, such as helping with dinner preparation and helping with bedtime for their sibling. All children can participate in providing input about family values and planning family vacations. By recording each family members' participation in building the team's cohesiveness, each family member will feel that he or she will have an impact on the outcome.

Once the family plan has been created it is critical that parents present it to the children in a positive, unified manner. If children detect there is discord between the parents or when one parent is not completely committed to the process, the children will not be committed to the process.

While parents must be in charge and united in developing, implementing, overseeing, and monitoring the plan, to create a team approach, remain open to your children's ideas and suggestions—they may have worthwhile suggestions to offer and if you decide to include their contributions, they will be more committed to staying on track. As your children get older, you can work together to set the goals. This will provide your children with a great sense of pride when goals they set are achieved and will help them to establish the skills that will be necessary to set goals of their own in school, at home, at work, and in life.

Both parents should be available to discuss and renegotiate when a change is required due to circumstance or if there is a shift in priority regarding goals or objectives. In a single parent family, it may be beneficial to get input from extended family and friends. Discuss your parenting plan and style with colleagues and share your frustrations when your approach is not working. Observe other families and see if the interactions they have with their children might work effectively with your own children.

When establishing the family routine, use the aforementioned short- and long-term goals to prioritize and establish your daily and overall life plan. Relying on the specific goals you have for each child and for the family as a whole will help you to manage your daily activities. As you achieve a goal, take a moment to pat yourself—or your partner or children—on the back before moving on to the next goal.

Including Your Support Team in Your Plan

When dealing with a complex family situation you will always need a "backup plan" to support your routine daily and weekly tasks and short-term objectives. This plan should include support team members that you can call on to help you keep your plan in motion if you are ill or if an unexpected circumstance occurs that prevents you from meeting your objectives or your children's. There will also be times when you may not be able to give each child their individual time, but while one child is attending a therapy session, you should make the most of the time you have with another child. When one child is in school, try to find some time to have fun with another. If grandma is around, or your relatives are visiting, help them plan a special activity, like going to the zoo. Rather than adding to the chaos, these people could provide the coverage you need to spend time on a ride with one child while the rest of the group is visiting the monkey exhibit.

If you share your short term plan with close members of your team, they will know what is required and be more prepared to jump in and help out when needed in a way that keeps things moving consistently. You can also include their participation or contribution in some of your planning and goal setting, and they can implement the goals they help you set.

Providing Flexible Structure

Whether it is a home with one child or many, all children need to feel that there is some semblance of order in their lives. Creating this blueprint will help in establishing routines that provide this order. As the parent of a special needs family, there will be many times when plans go awry and that is when you must rely on your instincts to know when to go with the flow temporarily or just wing it until you can get things back on track.

This requires engaging in "flexible structure." While this sounds like an oxymoron, it means that you should adhere to your plans but be willing and able to bend and flex when circumstances warrant it.

Most children, especially children with special needs thrive on routine and feel more comfortable knowing what to expect and when. Children are more productive when they have routines and will quickly become accustomed to having a set schedule for major activities, such as waking up in the morning, leaving for school, engaging in extracurricular activities, as well as mealtimes, bath time, homework, and playtimes (which should occur at roughly the same time each day). In fact, some are quick to point out or act out when a routine is changed or disrupted.

However, all children have good days and bad ones too. There may be days when any one of your children can not or will not follow the routine they followed the day before, which throws theirs—and everyone else's—schedule off kilter. Perhaps a child is ill or feels sad or moody or perhaps something external arises that impacts *your* life. Whatever occurs, on those days, you must be flexible. Depending on the ages and personalities of the children in the home, that flexibility may apply only to the child with special needs or to the child who cannot adapt to the circumstances. As the parent, you must decide when to give in and when it is essential to adhere to your routine. And, if you have a child who cannot deal with a lack of structure, you may have to implement a routine just for that child.

Weigh each situation and evaluate the pros and cons. For example, if your children are engrossed in a group activity and everyone is getting along, don't feel that at a certain time you must stop the fun. This would be a good time to evaluate the importance of moving on to the next activity, even if it is mealtime or bedtime, and determining whether the value of "just five more minutes" of meaningful family time outweighs the need to move on. If you allow these activities to linger, remain alert so that you know when it is time to move on to the next activity.

You can also teach your children the concept of flexible structure and time management. In dealing with young children or a child that has a hard time with transitions, give a five or ten minute warning before moving to a new activity. Whether you are leaving a friend's house or finishing an art project, this warning gives everyone, including you, ample opportunity to wrap up and switch gears. If you have a child who is particularly rigid or has difficulty accepting change, he or she may require more time than the others or even an incentive to move on.

If any of your children have difficulty or act out due to a temporary change in their routine, find a way to explain why the change or adjustment is being made and when you anticipate things will be back to "normal." If the change becomes a new routine, explain why.

Most of all, practice what you preach. As previously mentioned, some days even the best laid plans will go awry. Rather than get frustrated over changes in schedules and routines that you cannot control just roll with it.

Family Decision-making

As children grow and mature, there will be opportunities for them to develop and practice good decision-making skills. This can begin by encouraging young children to choose what clothing to wear, what to have for dinner, and which afterschool activities to participate in.

In a special needs family however, many decisions must take into account the needs of and impact on the child with special needs. To maintain a balance and keep any potential resentment at bay when circumstances need to tip in the direction of the child with special needs, inviting the siblings into some reasonable decision-making conversation may be helpful.

These decisions should involve a family discussion about each child's opinion, preferences, and the pros and cons of each decision. One child's needs should not outweigh another's and this includes the child with special needs. Present certain guidelines—perhaps by jotting down a list of items and options shared by everyone—and try to remain neutral so that the children do not feel pressured in one direction or the other. Each child can make a selection from a given list that falls within the parameters of what will work best for the family.

Whenever it is appropriate, the child with special needs should be included in family decisions as well. This helps the other children feel that all family members are equal and respected. And if a decision is made to leave the child with special needs behind, there should be some balance or opportunity to include that child at a later time.

Children who grow up in a home in which decisions are discussed rather than dictated to them learn to use good judgment in making more significant decisions later on. By including your children in the process, especially as they get older, you will find that they will be more inclined to follow through and become less rebellious.

Provide your children with choices and involve them in the decisions that are age-appropriate for them. For example, when you have a child who has difficulty with time management, especially with homework, take the time to discuss the assignments and the amount of time the child thinks it will take to complete each task. Help the child make choices about the order of completing those assignments, perhaps alternating between an easy assignment and a more difficult one. Your child could set short-term goals when completing a long-term assignment and include those tasks in the daily routine. When your children are older, this same method of guidance and prioritization will work for choosing activities and responsibilities that will fit into the family's routine.

Once the goals are set and the tasks are achieved, review and ac-knowledge the successes. Something that worked well today may also be effective in the future.

Though many aspects of raising a family that includes a child with special needs are chaotic and out of your control, having a plan and man-aging your family with forethought and specific guidelines will make the experience more tolerable and manageable. Establishing a written plan and specific achievable goals will help you organize your life and the many moving pieces, and give you the sense that you are moving in a positive direction.

As CEO of your family, you will be required to oversee all major decisions but do so in consultation with your spouse, partner, or other family members who you rely on for support.

Once you have written both short- and long-term goals, refer to them frequently to identify those that were achieved, those that require revision, and those that may be unattainable. If you determine that a goal is unattainable, try to revise it or replace it with a more realistic goal. Each time you achieve a goal, however small, take pride in your success. Share your pride with your family and friends so that they appreciate the family's accomplishments.

Try to be realistic in setting your goals and not feel defeated if some goals prove to be unachievable. This is not a failure but rather, a chance to readdress and try again at a later time.

Summary Points
- Become the CEO of your family by creating a plan that includes short- and long-terms goals.
- Consider each parents approach to parenting and work together to reinforce each other's strengths.
- If your parenting styles don't mesh, find ways to reconcile your differences through compromise and those viewpoints and values you do share.
- Spend time considering and setting goals for yourself, your children, and your family.
- Set achievable and realistic goals for each family member and assess your goals frequently to determine whether they are attainable.
- When possible, include children and support team members in the process of setting and implementing goals.
- Routines provide comfort and structure, especially for children, but try to be flexible when necessary.

- Find age appropriate ways to include your children in family decision-making.

Part III: Raising Children Together in a Special Needs Family

Chapter 6: Understanding Your Children's Experience with a Special Needs Sibling

It is important to consider the impact that a sibling with special needs can have on your children. Chances are you did not grow up with a sibling that required as much parental attention and you may not fully understand what your children are experiencing. You may have vied for your parents' attention or felt out of place among your peers at school, but your overall childhood experiences were different. Be conscious of what your children may be feeling or dealing with and let them know that you want to understand and learn from their experiences.

Explaining the Concept of "Special Needs" to Children of Any Age

We help our children comprehend the world they experience through shadowing them and labeling. We teach babies to speak by labeling the items they encounter such as, "bottle," and "car" and help young toddlers convey that they are "sad," or "happy."

When discussing the sibling's disability, explain the child's abilities and challenges in terms that are age appropriate. Providing this language early and often, helps the child learn to incorporate the concepts into their own thought process so they can understand and accept the sibling's condition and limitations. Provide enough information to clarify their concerns without overwhelming them. As your children mature, you can broaden your explanations and information.

- **Preschoolers:** A preschool child may not have the terms to express their feelings verbally, and may instead express themselves through their play or behavior. If you see a change in their behavior or interactions with their sibling, you may want to start a very rudimentary discussion about the differences in their sibling as compared to their friend's sibling. Younger children tend to be self-centered and may not seem to notice the differences but they are probably more aware than they seem. Using concrete examples and simple terms will help your child begin the process of acknowledging the differences. You might say, "your sister doesn't know how to talk but she does understand the things you say and really likes it when you sing to her."

- **Elementary School Children:** At an elementary school age, children are able to classify items into groups and they may become acutely aware of the fact that their sibling does not fit in. They may have exposure to classmates who have disabilities and be more informed than you realize, but this may lead to some confusion if they cannot identify the dissimilarities between their sibling's and peer's disabilities. Help them identify the differences in terms of strengths and weaknesses. Because they tend to be very concrete, give specific information that will contribute to their understanding of their sibling and not more than they can handle.

- **Adolescents:** Adolescents are more acutely aware of differences because they are trying desperately to establish their own identity and figure out their present and future roles. They may seek out information independently through online resources, and this may be confusing. Offer to help them sort through the information. Many children at this age, especially boys, tend to keep their emotions inside, or act out in other ways rather than address their feelings. Try to be accurate in the information you provide and convey information that will be reassuring. Share information that reflects their sibling's progress and help them include their friends in interactions with their sibling.

In general, provide explanations often and in more detail as your children mature or when they inquire. Don't overwhelm them with too much information or provide information when they are not ready to receive it. As they become more knowledgeable about their sibling's situation they will also become more adept at explaining the circumstances to friends and others outside the home.

"It's Not Your Fault"

It is important to convey that while you cannot always offer an explanation as to how or why a brother or sister was born with or acquired a disability, no one is to blame. Emphasizing this frees the siblings from feeling that they should be able to improve the situation and alleviates any guilt they may have about not being the one who has the disability or limitations.

Your children should also be encouraged to view their sibling as a whole person, rather than a person with a disability. This requires effort on your part, especially when the limitations are obvious. You should encourage your children to focus on each other's strengths. By pointing out the positive attributes and expressing your pride in each child's accomplishments, you can teach them to value themselves and to value one another.

The Impact of Birth Order

The topic of personality and birth order has been researched extensively, but there is little research regarding the impact of birth order in a home with a child with special needs.

I have found that there are differences between the experiences of siblings that are older and those that are younger than the child with special needs. In general, the reactions that children have to their special sibling will depend on their individual personalities, the personality and level of disability of the child with special needs, and the ways in which parents handle and relate to each child in the family.

All children have a period of adjustment upon the arrival of a new sibling. Some children are nurturing and accepting while others feel jealous and upset. Every child must acclimate to sharing their attention and their world with their parents. However, if the new child has special needs, the parents may have a more difficult time adjusting to the circumstances and added responsibilities, and this may affect the parent-child relationship. These circumstances may strain the sibling relationship as well.

Younger siblings tend to adjust more easily because they often enter the world *after* their parents are already dealing with, and hopefully managing, the sibling's needs. As this is the only family life they know, it feels normal to them at first. However, as they grow older and realize the situation is long term, they may experience a latent period of adjustment many years later.

Older siblings may be more challenged. Depending on their ages, they may feel a sense of disruption and change to the status quo, leading to negative behaviors or withdrawal. Some children may never accept their sibling's differences.

Try to be open minded and receptive to any and all reactions that your children might experience, whether sadness, frustration, anger or jealousy. Encourage them to express their feelings so that you can understand and provide the support and guidance they require. If they have difficulty expressing or sharing those feelings, you might consider finding a therapist that could help them express their feelings in a safe environment.

The Impact of Personality and Gender Differences

Children have diverse personalities and, as such, will react and respond to one another in unique ways. There are times when everybody will get along and other times when they won't. If the child with special needs has a pleasant and easygoing disposition, the siblings are often drawn to that child, and may adjust and relate well. If the siblings are easygoing and flexible, too, interactions are likely to be pleasant and positive.

However, if either the child with special needs or their sibling has a more demanding personality and requires more of the family's energy, this can create an unbalanced situation. Siblings may act up to gain the attention they feel may be lacking. Moreover, when the attention is focused on the sibling, a more demanding child with special needs may have a meltdown to refocus the parents' attention back on him or her.

Keep in mind that your responses to these challenging relationships may be the most significant factor in determining whether these difficult dynamics are reinforced or whether the children learn alternative ways to react. As previously mentioned, focusing on positive behavior and minimizing your reactions to negative behavior will have an influence on your children's reactions when similar circumstances arise at a later time.

Gender may also be of influence. Girls tend to be more emotion-focused and usually wear their hearts on their sleeve. They may also be very verbal and express their reactions openly. Most girls tend to be more responsible and nurturing, which is often praised and reinforced by the adults in their life. As such, they may naturally take on—and take pride in—playing a more supportive role in caring for the sibling with special needs.

In general, boys tend to be more self-contained in their emotions and coping methods. They often avoid talking about their feelings, and tend to either act on their emotions or to become withdrawn. Boys may seem completely oblivious, going about their lives as if there is nothing that concerns them. Depending on their age and gender, your son may need assistance labeling his feelings and talking through his reactions. He may be more willing to communicate his feelings when you identify your own.

In relating to their sibling with special needs, both boys and girls may be protective and defend the sibling against outside ridicule or bullying. They may find unusual common ground through telling jokes, watching TV/movies together, or playing games or sports, and this could become the primary basis of their relationship. Yet, at other times, they may feel weird, awkward, or embarrassed and unsure how to behave or respond. If you sense their discomfort, taking the time to talk about ways to encourage a relationship, no matter how small, will plant a seed that could easily grow over time.

Of course, many of these generalities may not apply specifically to your children. You may find that your daughter dislikes or resents having any responsibility toward her sibling or that your son is completely committed to the role. There are many brothers that rise to the occasion, taking on very nurturing roles and enjoying the praise they receive from their positive interactions with their siblings, and sisters who are initially nurturing and then become more self- or peer-focused in later years.

Regardless of their reactions, allow your children to be themselves and come to terms in their own time. You may find that as they get older, siblings change their perspective, but as long as you are accepting of their reactions, they will be less resentful toward their sibling with special needs.

How Children Handle Their Emotions

When he was in high school, Jason wrote an essay that conveyed his experiences of growing up with a brother with special needs. He described how obtaining his driver's license was a highlight of his teenage years because it gave him a great deal of independence, but he also felt guilty because he realized his younger brother would never learn to drive.

I was touched by my son's self-awareness and his willingness to share his feelings openly. His recapitulation of this milestone reinforced the importance of acknowledging and validating the feelings that the siblings have throughout their lives. Rather than holding those feelings inside or keeping them a secret, your children should be encouraged to discuss them with you and with each other.

Your children will experience a myriad of emotions. Even at a very young age, many children may share their parents' worries and concerns about their sibling with special needs. Many children lack the language and cognitive skills to truly understand their sibling's issues and may internalize their stress in order to avoid adding burden to an already stressful family situation. Some may feel ashamed of the anger and guilt they feel and this may have a significant impact on their self-esteem. Others may turn those feelings on other people in their life, including other siblings, parents, friends, and teachers. Over time, these emotions may lead to depression, anxiety, or somatic complaints.

It is important to note that the characteristics of depression may be manifested as irritability rather than sadness in some children. They may have trouble sleeping, lose interest in activities, or become withdrawn. As such, whenever you recognize a significant change in your child's mood or behavior you should try to identify whether they have specific issues or concerns. Most children, especially young children won't be able to acknowledge or articulate their concerns and may need your assistance to put their feelings into words.

Here are some tips that will help:

1. **Communicate in a way your children will understand.**
   Finding the appropriate words is often the most difficult challenge. When dealing with a preschooler, you might state that "your heart hurts" or that "you feel sad". Acknowledge the feelings and encourage the child to talk about them. Focus on expe-

riences that make the child feel angry or sad so that they have concrete examples that will help them differentiate. It is also helpful to show your happy feelings to these concrete learners and praise them for ways that they are a good sister or brother. When your older children ask questions, try to be as direct and truthful as possible. Give them a straightforward explanation, presenting the information in a way that they will understand. If they ask a simple question, give a simple answer—don't overwhelm them with details or a lengthy explanation that is way over their heads. For example, when explaining communication issues, you might want to state that their sister "doesn't always have the words to let us know what she wants but she definitely has wants and needs just as you do." Even when they are young, your other children will want to know that when they are sensing something is wrong, someone else can confirm it for them. They are very attuned to their environment and can sense when they or someone they care about is being treated differently.

2. **Strive to be truthful and sincere.**
   Don't lie to your children because they are very savvy and can tell when you are misleading them. If you start to hedge or become unclear, they may fill in the blanks with their own inaccurate explanations. Many of the families that face significant issues with the siblings, are overprotective or have minimized the reality of how difficult it can be to have a sibling with special needs. The more honest you are, the better prepared your child will be to face the daunting reality that there are many people they will encounter in life who have a limited capacity to accept differences.

3. **Reach out and touch.**

   Teach your children that while words are essential for strong interpersonal relationships, touch is important, too. Express your
   care, concern, and love physically through touch—hugs, kisses,
   or a gentle, reassuring stroke of a hand. This will be beneficial
   to the sibling with special needs, particularly when there is a
   communication issue. As they learn to show affection through
   tickling and giggling together, they will find common ground and
   establish a bond.

4. **Provide your children with the tools that will encourage interaction.**

   Whether it is through toys or activities, be available to facilitate
   the interaction and then pull back as your children learn to interact on their own. As they find common ground, their relationship will flourish.

When children are supported and given the language to address their
own and their sibling's issues, they will develop an ability to discuss their
emotions under other circumstances and this will have a positive impact
on their self-confidence, especially when times are challenging.

Most siblings of a child with special needs are hyper-vigilant. When
out in public, they are aware of the nasty stares and snide remarks far
more often than you are. During those situations, when you may be trying desperately to manage yet another public meltdown or tantrum from
your child with special needs, your other children are often left with nothing more to do than stare back at a by-passer with a disgusted look that
seems to be conveying, "What kind of parent are you? Can't you manage
your child?"

When the situation has passed, take the time to discuss your feelings
as a family and let your children know that you understand how bad or

uncomfortable they feel. In time, rather than dwelling on or perpetuating these feelings, they can simply share and acknowledge them and then move on.

Do not bubble wrap your child's world or try to shield them from reality. It is not your responsibility to protect them from the truth, but rather, to protect them from becoming devastated by it. This is not to say that your children must be informed at all times, and certainly, you must consider their age both in determining what information to share and how best to present it to them.

It is important to acknowledge the reality of your situation and to share the feelings that go with it. Sharing will help to build a positive relationship between you and your children and the children with one another as they begin to identify common emotions. You should also give your children the opportunity to express the feelings they may have about their sibling (or his behavior), good and bad, without judgment.

Acknowledge and support any and all feelings, but most importantly, let your children know that it is safe for them to share their feelings with you and with other people. Doing so will help them to temper any potential anger and alleviate stress and frustration. Through this process, you will come to understand your children from a new perspective, which will help you be a more enlightened parent.

Redirecting Displaced Feelings

In many families, children often direct their feelings toward a less threatening or more vulnerable family member. However, in the case of a special needs family, children are usually protective of their sibling with special needs. They are reluctant to direct their negative feelings at that sibling who they may perceive as defenseless and unfortunate. As such, they are more likely to direct their emotions toward each other, you, or another caregiver.

When the heat of the moment has passed, take the time to help your child discover their true feelings and to consider other ways to express and discuss them with you, rather than at you, in the future.

When Feelings Prove Difficult to Handle

Growing up in a family with a child with special needs may yield many different emotions, which can have significant effects on each of the children. These responses can not only affect their relationship with other family members, but also could affect their ability to form strong social relationships in later years.

Some children feel trapped and helpless or guilty. They may even withdraw, further exacerbating their feelings of isolation. They may also feel responsible for their sibling and may not be aware of the impact of this burden. Over time, they may become depressed and these sad feelings may become all consuming.

Other children may become angry and hostile, and may not limit those feelings to their family members. Often, these individuals have not fully accepted the devastating feelings of loss and disappointment, choosing instead to blame others for their situation. They may unconsciously damage relationships or create situations where people choose to avoid them. In doing so, they often rationalize that people are cruel and uncaring and this is further justification for the harsh way they are treated.

Some siblings suppress their emotions, holding it together most of the time. But when they eventually express their true feelings, their reactions may be rather extreme. It is helpful to give them different ways to express their feelings and perhaps to engage them in some positive physical activity to release some of the tension.

Support groups might help, particularly for a child who is both verbal and social. However, many siblings are uncomfortable in these settings or find support groups to be too broad to address their experiences.

Support groups can be helpful when they involve sharing activities rather than feelings with others. For some children, hearing other siblings voice their feelings may cause them to become more depressed or withdrawn. But when they have opportunities to engage in fun and enriching activities together, they eventually come to recognize the common bonds and draw support from the other siblings that share their experiences.

If you perceive that any of your children needs support beyond what you are personally able to provide, you should consider finding a therapist that has an understanding of the specific issues that siblings in a special needs family face, and can help your child express their feelings. It is most beneficial to establish individual therapy for each child because the issues are often as diverse as their individual experiences and perceptions of the problems.

The Importance of Open Communication

As stated earlier, and worth restating, one of the most valuable lessons for your children is the importance of communicating both positive and negative feelings. Expressing resentment, rage, exasperation, disappointment, animosity, jealousy, and frustration are all just as normal as conveying love, devotion, and appreciation.

By leaving the door of communication open in your home, you give your children permission to discuss how they feel when they are ready to express themselves without the fear of shame or embarrassment.

Whether part of a family discussion, in the moment, or one-on-one, giving your children the sense that you care about how they feel and what they can contribute is important to their development.

You may want to schedule family meetings to address problems and discuss feelings. Children will come to see that a family meeting is a safer and more equitable environment for addressing their concerns. It also allows them the opportunity to express their feelings when they are not in the heat of an argument.

Reinforce positive interactions between your children and let them know how much it means to you when they communicate well and get along. Focusing on the differences in personalities and interests among the siblings rather than the obvious aspects of a child's special needs, will encourage self-awareness and acceptance.

By engaging your children in an open dialogue, you can build their confidence and allow them to feel comfortable presenting their views and feelings. The practice they get in sharing their feelings and ideas at home helps them learn to communicate their personal experiences outside of the home as well, and will go a long way in helping them to become a better friend and mate.

Summary Points

- Explain the concept of a sibling's special needs and behaviors in terms that your children understand and make sure they know that they are not at fault.
- Birth order and gender may have some impact on how children relate to their sibling with special needs, but each child's personality and acceptance will have a great impact as well.
- Similar to their parents' experiences, children feel a vast array of emotions and should be encouraged to express their feelings at all times in a communicative and non-judgmental environment.
- A child's reactions may change over time. Be aware of changes, especially in behavior and mood that may indicate the need for additional support.
- Some children may act out or displace their frustrations towards others and away from the sibling they perceive as most vulnerable. Help them find acceptable ways to share their emotions.
- If children have difficulty adjusting, support groups and counseling may be helpful.

Chapter 7: Relationship Building: The Triumphs and Challenges

Raising children together will have a fair amount of challenges even in the best of circumstances. Include a child with special needs to the mix and you have an extra and complex layer. Establishing relationships between the children may take time and patience.

Regardless of their age, many children with special needs are perceived as the youngest member in a family and are treated as such. Many siblings tend to treat the child with special needs with "kid gloves." They can become extremely protective and take measures to keep them from being picked on or hurt by others around them both inside and outside the home. Sometimes, rather than becoming a mate, a sibling takes on the qualities of a parent or guardian. Though this protective relationship may be beneficial since it minimizes conflict between the siblings, you will want your children to experience the worry-free innocence of childhood.

On the other side, it may be difficult to engage the child with special needs in a relationship because of the specific aspects of their disability. A child with autism, for example, may not be socially connected or able to communicate sufficiently to interact. These children may also have developmental delays in which their abilities and interests are significantly below their chronological age.

There are great rewards for all your children when siblings can encourage their brother or sister to establish and maintain good play skills. Having the patience to find common ground will help both siblings learn the value of perseverance. The opportunities to interact in meaningful play activities will go a long way in increasing the bond that these siblings share later on in life.

Ways to Engage

It may be beneficial to model and teach your children basic skills to engage their brother or sister in meaningful play activities. Children at a young age can learn to gain their sibling's attention and to communicate in brief and simple terms that the sibling will understand. Older siblings could share interests in music and crafts, that involve minimal language, yet can be interactive.

At a very young age, children engage in parallel play, playing next to each other and even doing the same activity without interacting. This initial type of play is very meaningful for children with special needs. By observing their siblings engaging in fun activities, they can learn the pleasure that play can provide and mimic even the most rudimentary skills. For example, a child with a language delay may not be able to learn the words to a song but might be able to hum along. The child might learn the chorus through repetition or some basic hand gestures and dance steps they can engage in with their sibling. Their siblings, even those who are very young, enjoy the opportunity to serve as a model and enjoy the attention they receive from their sibling's companionship.

Some children have physical or motor skill related challenges, while others have behavioral or emotional difficulties that get in the way of their play. However, there are ways to overcome these limitations so that your children can find common ground. For example, you can assist by obtaining items such as books, musical instruments, bubbles and arts and crafts supplies, that will initiate play, and encourage the siblings to find ways to interact with one another.

Watching a movie, listening to music, taking a walk, playing with a family pet, and playing computer or video games, are all ways that children with diverse abilities can play together. The children can also interact while creating crafts, cooking in the kitchen, or doing puzzles. Outdoor play, especially riding bikes, swimming, shooting a basketball, swinging in a park and playing catch tend to be less competitive and therefore may be a good medium for sibling interaction.

Team-related activities can work too. When playing board games, for example, it may be helpful for the children (or family members, when included) to pair up in teams so that stronger players can help their partner have the chance to win the game.

Though it may be necessary to make accommodations, such as having the child with special needs engage in the activity for a shorter period of time, or having the siblings serve as the teacher, you will be surprised at how flexible your children can be, especially once they learn that playing together can be great fun!

Being a Good Team Member

Teamwork is a good way to foster strong relationships among your children. All children, including the child with special needs, should be encouraged to participate in team activities and to contribute their ideas and thoughts to group discussions.

Here are a few ways that you can build team skills with and among your children:

- **Having dinner dates:** Set up small dinner tables in a family room and divide your group into "dinner dates." You may decide to assign teams or have captains that pick their team members. Each team can help prepare and serve dinner, as well as clean up. Even for a small family, an occasional intimate dinner of two or three can be a fun alternative to the larger family dinner. You may want to plan variations on the menu based on each group's preferences. For example, one table may be having pasta with a tomato-based sauce and the other may have a white sauce and vegetables. It's easy to prepare one pot of pasta and two sauces, so that each group's dinner is special. The children can create team names and decorate menus together. You may decide that the children will eat together at one small table while parents dine alone at another table, or each child can pick a parent that they want to eat with for that particular meal. After some intimate conversation and alone time, the whole family can then join together to enjoy a special dessert.

- **Choosing team building activities:** During mealtime or at another time, assign a team building activity. Have each team or group work on their specific goals. When planning a family trip, you may want to collect brochures and pictures and have the children select their preferred destination or plan specific family activities during the trip. An older sibling could help gather the information on the Internet and then the younger siblings could submit their order of prioritization for the available activities. Working together to plan the events will add to the camaraderie and excitement, both before and during the trip. Encourage the children to plan a special breakfast for Mother's Day or shop together to purchase a gift for Dad's birthday. These activities will help the children learn to express their own preferences and appreciate that their siblings have a great deal to offer.

- **Creating collaboration spaces:** Set up a picnic in your backyard or at a park and use that relaxed atmosphere as a place to discuss family relationships. Take the family out to the mall to spend time together. You could set up a scavenger hunt in either of these settings, giving family members the opportunity to spend time together seeking out a hidden treasure or special prize. After finding several clues, the final meeting place could be at the ice cream stand in the mall or back at the picnic basket where dessert will be waiting. This may be an opportunity for a younger child or the child with special needs to shine if they are able to lead the group through the hunt.

- **Encouraging job shadowing opportunities:** You could also apply the concepts of workplace team building to your family. Following someone through their workday is a great way for people from different departments to gain knowledge and understanding of the other employees experiences and responsibilities. You can apply this at home by giving your children the opportunity to shadow you to see all that you accomplish in a day. Similarly, a child with special needs could shadow a sibling through their day or help cheer from the stands when their sibling scores a goal. The sibling could shadow the child with special needs to cheer them on during school or therapy and provide valuable reinforcement when they accomplish a new task. The value of sibling support is remarkably encouraging and may go farther than the support of parents, teachers and peers!

- **Encouraging mentoring:** One-on-one mentoring is another approach to team building. During the mentoring process, each child learns new skills and bonds with the mentor— parent, grandparent, or sibling—at the same time. You may find that your children have special talents that they can teach each family member through one-to-one time. Gather the supplies and have your child teach everyone how to make a bracelet or decorate cookies. It may be fascinating to find that your children can adapt the tasks for their sibling with special needs so that they can enjoy the activity together. Your child with special needs may have certain interests that they can share with other family members. For example, if a child is a master at Lego building or puzzles purchase different kits that they could work on with family members.

Sibling Rivalry

Rivalry between siblings is an issue that creeps up in every family at some point, no matter how well the children may appear to get along. The surprising reality is that children do not naturally play well together. This is another skill that they must learn.

There are many factors that contribute to sibling rivalry and it's not just about competition. Children observe parents' interactions and learn from them. Parents who are frequently in conflict with one another have children who fight. Children who observe a parent treating a spouse with little respect tend to be disrespectful to their siblings. When parents demonstrate compromise and respect, siblings learn to resolve their differences and usually get over the conflicts.

Any parent that tells you their children never argue or disagree is either lying or choosing to be oblivious to their children's interactions. Fighting is actually a sign that your children are being "healthy, normal siblings." Sibling rivalry is an essential element of growing up that allows children to learn how to express themselves, to discover their independence, and recognize how to share all the things in the world that are important to them.

Research has shown that siblings fight approximately ten minutes out of every hour. Only children learn to interact socially through the rejection they face from their peers when they interact inappropriately.

Siblings have the advantage of knowing they can fight with each other without fear of rejection.

Living day in and day out in a household among family members with diverse personalities and needs is bound to create various bumps in the road. Familiarity and comfort, while providing emotional security, can also lead to children acting and speaking in uncensored ways. They may not realize that their words and actions may be hurtful to someone close to them or they may not care.

There are many reasons that all children experience sibling rivalry but many of these may be more pronounced in the home of a special needs family. When the parents are experiencing stress over the care of the child with special needs or, for that matter, any conflict in their life that takes priority, it is natural for the children's different needs and identities to have an impact on the way that they relate to one another. Despite your best intentions to teach your children to wait for the attention to be focused on them, they are still children and having patience will be very difficult for them at times. When your children feel they are being neglected or overlooked, regardless of their age, they may create a conflict with another family member, usually with a sibling, to redirect their parents' attention back on them.

Sometimes they just act out because they are feeling bad, not necessarily about anything specific. They believe they will feel better if someone else feels as bad as they do.

Conflict between siblings may be about adjusting to sharing a space and possessions with someone else and it is an essential part of growing up. If your living quarters are small, give each child their own space as well as their own personal belongings that they do not have to share.

You may find that one child becomes jealous if you share interests with another child and sibling rivalry may result. As parents, we know that we should avoid playing favorites, but a positive rapport we have with one child, may be obvious to the others. Children may also resent a parent who spends more time with one child or gives more responsibility to another, more mature but younger child.

In a home with a child with special needs, the rivalry may be more about having to compete for parents' attention. Even though they know it is in their sibling's best interest, there may be times when that doesn't matter to them or that their feelings seem more important. They may choose to direct their frustration toward another sibling because they feel guilty about directing it at their parents or the sibling that requires more care.

You can remedy this by setting up a weekly schedule that gives each child time to spend with each parent individually. This time does not always have to involve doing "fun" activities—it could be as simple as taking one child along to the grocery store.

There may be frequent feelings of jealousy on the part of the child with special needs who feels that their siblings have opportunities and abilities that they do not. It may be helpful to identify this issue as an underlying cause of conflict between siblings and to help each child recognize and embrace what makes them unique. Encouraging your children to point out and validate positive traits and abilities in each other will pave the way towards appreciating each other rather than feeling jealous or resentful.

It is natural for children of all ages to be competitive with one of their siblings. There are many adults who are still competing with their siblings, whether it's about status, education, accomplishments, or even for their parents' attention and affection.

The issues that lead to sibling rivalry in a home with a child with special needs are complex because there may be language, developmental, and emotional issues that contribute to the conflict. These conflicts cannot be ignored or they will escalate and create a greater schism in the relationship that the siblings share. Encouraging communication and comfort in expressing feelings in a special needs family leads to discussion, which then leads to understanding.

With regard to the conflicts that arise among siblings, it is important to thwart any physical fighting or abusive interaction. Children should understand that although there may be times that they do not get along, causing any physical harm is completely unacceptable.

When conflicts escalate and one child can't get along with the others, watch for recurring patterns of behavior. Address the issues separately, in a quiet, calm manner, with that child. You may be able to put certain schedules or plans in place to avoid these conflicts completely. For example, if your children often fight about sharing special toys (i.e., a new Lego kit from Grandma), you could rotate the schedule so that each child has priority access to those toys on designated days. That would mean that if a conflict arises over that toy on a given day, the child with priority access gets to play with the toy first and when he or she is done the other child would have their turn. Over time, the allure will decrease and so will the conflicts.

Teach your children to identify their own and their sibling's trigger points. For example, if you have a child with a temper who frequently loses his cool, you may want to speak to the other children, at a quieter time, about how they can tell when that sibling may be about to blow, and then encourage them to walk away so that the situation does not escalate. If the situation gets really out of control with any one child, consider seeking professional help.

As they mature, children should know that it is their responsibility to work out their rivalries and conflicts as best they can. You will find that as they learn to work out their differences they find more ways to share their similar interests and enjoy spending time together. Learning to live together and appreciate one another will help your children develop the fidelity and loyalty that exists between siblings who know they can rely on one another throughout their life.

Resolving Sibling Conflicts

Learning to resolve conflict is important and is most effective when your children can begin to practice those skills in the safety of their own home with someone close and trusted. Through resolving conflicts with their siblings, your children will learn to mediate on their own behalf and accept compromise. They will also come to know that their brother or sister will continue to be their siblings even after the fight is over.

It is almost impossible to find a conflict where one side is one hundred percent right and the other one hundred percent wrong. In the overwhelming majority of cases, each person is a contributor to the conflict. Through conflict resolution, your children also learn to become more sensitive to the thoughts and feelings that another person may be experiencing. Taking another person's perspective and appreciating his position is a very valuable skill that all children should learn.

In teaching your children to resolve their conflicts you can show them that they have a much better chance of resolving their differences if they can examine, with honesty, the part they played in the dispute.

The children in a home with a sibling with special needs are more attuned to peoples' weaknesses, including their own. They may have more courage to put aside their ego and take responsibility for the part that they may have instigated. Once each child has taken ownership of the conflict, and each has an ability to see the other person's point of view, the resolution is usually easier to attain.

It is best to teach your children to resolve their conflicts when they are young and the issues are less significant. The willingness to give something up for the sake of achieving a resolution is a lot easier when the siblings are fighting over a toy than when they are fighting over the attention of a parent or best friend. Their young minds are more open to resolving the issues and it is easier to teach the lessons when the issues are less emotional.

Taking a timeout to calm down works well for children and adults. Rather than breaking up a fight between family members, it may be best to take a break when things get heated to allow each person to compose his feelings and gather his thoughts before entering into a negotiation.

If you realize that a child's fuse is getting short, remove that child from the situation. If you are the one that is close to a breaking point and there is no one else present to step in, separate the children by giving them different activities that may be in different rooms. Once they have had the time to calm down, you can encourage them to get together to discuss their feelings and views.

Don't focus on who started the fight or who is to blame because both parties are usually responsible. It doesn't really matter who is more responsible.

When conflicts arise between your children, avoid being the mediator. It is best to try to remove yourself from the situation so that your children learn to work things out on their own and do not feel that you are taking sides. Your role should be more of a communicator rather than as a negotiator. Be available to help them communicate the reasons that the conflict developed and to teach them better ways to get their point across. When they are young or if they have a communication issue, you may have to help provide the words that reflect their feelings so that they could express themselves appropriately.

As your children evolve and change, the rivalries change too. When teaching conflict resolution, consider the developmental level of the participants, and their ability to understand and communicate the conflict. In a home with a child with special needs, it is even more important to help the siblings understand each other's developmental level and how that contributes to the conflict. Though the siblings may be close in age, their viewpoints may differ significantly based on their understanding.

For example, toddlers or the child with cognitive delay whose understanding is at an early developmental level are first learning about their own independence. They have trouble sharing because they believe that the focus is always on them and their needs. They have trouble seeing an argument from another person's perspective and are less likely to give anything up in an argument because they haven't learned to share or compromise.

School age children who are discovering the concepts of fairness and equality may not understand why one child, even a child with obvious limitations, requires or receives more attention than another. They may seem more sophisticated than a toddler but continue to see conflicts in black and white and will need help to see the grays. Since arguments often involve different people's perceptions of the same issue, they may have trouble acknowledging the subtleties of the conflict.

Teenagers who are focused on developing their individual identities and independence may have trouble connecting to the family and may choose to reject a family member rather than work through their differences. They may need your help to recognize the value of family and to appreciate the fact that relationships with family members usually last much longer than the relationships they form with their friends.

Aside from the developmental differences that may be present in sibling rivalries, each child comes to the family with a different disposition and ability to adapt. One child may be more set in his ways and another may be unable to see things from multiple perspectives. One child may be more independent and another child may be clingy. They may clash over their connection with one another because the independent child resents their sibling clinging to them. A laid back child may have conflict with a sibling who is overly bossy or pushy.

Younger siblings, though cute at first, may become more difficult to handle when they mimic an older brother or sister or insist on tagging along with them. The tolerance that an older sibling may have early on may diminish over time, particularly if that sibling is having a hard time dealing with the family situation or is facing some other stress outside of the house.

During those circumstances when you can recognize that a child's tolerance for a sibling is diminished, try to find ways to separate them, rather than require frequent interaction. You may find that the absence "makes the heart grow fonder," and that time spent apart helps your children want to spend more quality time with one another.

In general, if any sibling rivalries escalate to the point of concern or beyond your ability to help resolve, consider seeking professional help.

Working Together on Common Goals

There is a well-known social psychology experiment, in which children from different backgrounds were randomly assigned to two groups. The groups were then isolated from each other and, during that time, the group members developed a strong bond with one another. Later, when the groups were brought together, the children were competitive and antagonistic toward the members of the other group and defended the members of their own group.

In order to get all of the children to work together, the children were given a common goal to achieve. When working together on a shared project, all of the children, regardless of group, worked together harmoniously and established a common identity.

The siblings of a child with special needs already share a common goal—they are united by their unique family experience and the ways in which they have adapted to living together. These shared experiences enhance their relationship. Those who may have faced ridicule or ostracism by their peers are bonded by their experience and are often as protective and supportive of one another as they are with their sibling with special needs.

When fostering positive sibling engagement or even intervening when "kids are being kids" and not getting along as well as they should, you may find that setting up a situation that involves cooperation and collaboration will encourage camaraderie, and help to diffuse the conflicts. Simple tasks such a setting the table together can become fun activities. For example, challenge your children to create a centerpiece that fits the theme of the meal. Have them create place cards out of Legos or art supplies. At holiday times, the children can all help with decorating the house or stuffing and addressing holiday cards.

Working together presents opportunities for the siblings to recognize each other's strengths and gain satisfaction from completing a shared task. They may require help to find age-appropriate tasks for each child, including a role for the child with special needs, but once the task is assigned leave them to their own devices to complete the job. For example, have the children work together to plan and prepare a special family dinner or provide colored buckets and bins so that they can organize the playroom. Encourage all of the children to help with the laundry. They can sort through their clothes together, separating the darks and lights, load clothes into the washing machine and dryer, and even help with folding the clean clothes. Everyone can make an important contribution to completing tasks and the siblings learn the value of working cooperatively with their special brother or sister. Tasks are completed more quickly when everyone has a role and that means more time left to do fun activities together. Once the task is completed, the entire family could go outside for a friendly game of football on the lawn.

Encourage your children to express their appreciation to one another and to acknowledge each person's contribution. Even if conflicts arise while they work together, step aside and let them work it out. As long as no one is being physically hurt, let the arguments go until they reach their own resolution.

As children in a special needs family, these siblings develop a unique bond that cannot be replicated in any other interpersonal relationship. They tend to become protective of their sibling with special needs, and of one another. They become a unit and function as one, especially during the most difficult times. The support system that is created will influence all of their future relationships.

Cooperation and Compromise

Growing up in a home with a child with special needs provides many opportunities for cooperation and compromise. When the parents are working well together, the siblings observe the problem solving and compromise demonstrated and this becomes the hallmark of their positive social relationships.

The way parents resolve conflict with each other and with their children sets an example for the siblings to find a resolution for their own conflicts. If you and your partner tend to become aggressive or nasty, your children will model that. If you tend to withdraw from conflict, your children will likely pull away and be left feeling resentful with the conflict remaining unresolved.

You may want to practice talking through differences in a respectful and non-aggressive manner. For example, you might say, "I don't appreciate it when you speak to me that way" or "when you take that position it makes me feel as if my views are not important to you."

Teach your children to compromise and to recognize the value of other people's opinions and contributions. Use humor as a method to diffuse the situation and let your children see the lighter side of the situation as well.

Once the argument is resolved, convey the importance of maintaining a strong family bond and let your children know that although they may be very different and may argue, it doesn't mean that they are not loved equally.

Discuss how the situation can be dealt with differently in the future. It is important to talk about differences and the need to respect one another. Ultimately, if they care enough about each other they may be willing to give something up in order to help make the other person feel better.

Remember that the focus is not on the specific issue but rather about providing children with life skills that include resolving disputes, cooperation, compromise, teamwork, and caring about others. They are learning to value another person's perspective and to negotiate that which is important to them.

Show your children that you value the hard work that is necessary to resolve an issue and find a compromise. Don't let them quit or give up in the middle of a conflict resolution because the conflict will likely resurface repeatedly. By showing them that they can get through the problem and reach a resolution, even when it gets hard, they learn they can overcome other obstacles. They also learn that you believe in them, which gives them tremendous self worth.

As they get older, they will learn the importance of substituting aggressive behaviors with verbal expression. As they become better able to convey their feelings to you and to each other, conflict resolution will become more attainable.

If your children tend to fight about the same things, it is ideal to prevent those fights by resolving the conflicts before they happen. For example, if the fights are over video game playing time, set up a schedule. If the fights are over sharing a bedroom, establish some delineation of possessions and space. If the fights are over spending "alone time" with parents, schedule individual time for each child.

Though the fights between siblings may drive you crazy at times, through having conflicts and finding the resolution to them, your children will learn to compromise in the home and with outsiders. As your children learn to negotiate and compromise with one another, they discover what is truly important to them. This helps with future conflicts because they may be less inclined to engage in a struggle once they become aware of their priorities.

As the relationships and trust grow, they will recognize that their sibling will be there for them over time. Learning to cooperate with one another helps foster a lifelong relationship between siblings. They learn not to take one another for granted.

Summary Points
- Understand that sibling rivalry is natural. As children mature, they can gradually learn to work out their conflicts without parental intervention.
- Team building activities help children learn to appreciate and encourage one another rather than to compete and battle for parents' attention.
- Create and encourage team-building activities and allow all children to engage in a cooperative manner.
- Watch for recurring patterns and try to resolve or avoid those issues.
- If children have conflicts they cannot resolve, it may help to separate them for a time so all parties can have clarity.
- Once they have had the opportunity to collect their thoughts have the children talk through their feelings and help them to understand each parties perspective.
- Help a younger child or the child with special needs find the language to express his or her position but don't speak for them.
- By working together on common goals and activities, children's attention will be more focused on the tasks at hand, which will work to avoid or alleviate conflict.
- If there are certain conflicts that cannot be resolved or a child that has more difficulty with conflict resolution, consider seeking professional help.

- Working together provides more time for everyone to engage in fun activities.
- Learning to negotiate and compromise inside your home will provide your child with the important tools to become a better friend, employee, and mate.

Chapter 8: Setting Goals, Following Rules, and Ways to Discipline

The life of a parent with a child with special needs is filled with frequent doctors' appointments, sessions with therapists, and IEP (Individualized Education Program) meetings. We are frequently asked to record progress and change. For some, the improvement may be minimal and it is frustrating to realize how little has changed.

For others, the change may reflect a decline or a loss of previously acquired skills. It is especially difficult and devastating to watch your other children progress and mature while acknowledging that things aren't necessarily getting better for your child with special needs.

This experience may be as hard on your other children as it is on you. It is essential to remind your children that setbacks and lack of progress in the sibling's development is not uncommon, and that it is best to focus on and be proud of whatever progress is made. Celebrating the milestones achieved by each of your children should bring joy, not guilt. Small steps eventually lead to bigger accomplishments.

As part of your larger family "business plan" as covered in Chapter 5, set realistic goals that your children can meet so that they can take pride in their individual achievements. Start by setting smaller goals that can be accomplished in an hour or even in a few minutes, like completing an assignment or calling to thank grandma for a gift. As they meet these goals, they can take pride in their actions when they are checked off the list.

Encouraging children to help set goals or help you accomplish yours is another way to foster independence and build self-esteem. When out grocery shopping, for example, let younger children hold the grocery list and mark off the items as each one is put into the cart. With practice, children will learn to identify certain words and this will become an important step toward learning to read. As they get older, include them in planning dinners for the coming week by selecting recipes in cookbooks and organizing the shopping list of items needed. Involve all family members in planning a weekend outing or a family vacation.

The more involved your children are in planning and implementing tasks and activities, the more active and responsible they will become in the process. Planning, decision-making, and follow through are all essential skills for success and you can start teaching and modeling these skills at any age.

Establishing and Following Rules

With regard to setting rules, there is not a "one-size fits all" policy. In a home in which there is more than one child, including one facing many challenges, the rules and the consequences should be child-specific. That is not to say that there won't be some rules that apply to everyone, but you must also recognize and delineate rules that apply to each child.

You may establish a rule that all of your children must go to their rooms at a set time, so that you can have time for yourself or to spend together with your spouse. While in their room, children could be encouraged to engage in different activities, depending on their age. For example, the youngest child may be tucked into bed, another child may do something quiet like reading a book, and an older child might be expected to study for an exam.

You may decide to implement a rule that each child must complete homework on school nights, before pursuing other activities or watching TV. Since the children may have different assignments depending on their ages or abilities, one child may play or watch TV sooner or more than another. This may initially cause frustration among the child who still has homework or chores to complete, but in the end, everyone will learn that completing responsibilities means more leisure time to follow.

An older child, who takes more time to complete homework, may have an extended bedtime so that he or she has ample opportunity to develop other interest and hobbies. This may cut into the time that you and your spouse have together but it may also provide individual time with that child that wouldn't otherwise be available.

The rules for the child with special needs may be different and created to consider the child's disability. Children with developmental challenges may not be capable of following the same rules as the other children, and the siblings may perceive these differences as unfair. If this is the case, point out the areas where the children's rules are the same and remind your other children why their sibling is unable to comply.

You should try to establish a system that balances each child's needs and the family's ability to adapt. Be prepared to change the rules if you find that they no longer apply.

Managing Expectations and Responsibilities

Despite your greatest efforts to establish your position within the family and maintain the parent-child boundary, it is realistic to acknowledge that you may occasionally rely on the other children to help out, either by doing more for themselves or helping care for their sibling. Make sure they don't envision themselves in the role of parent.

In order to maintain the parent-child boundary that may at times be blurred by the circumstances, if you feel that a child is overstepping the boundaries do not hesitate to remind your children that you are the parent.

Though they may deny it, all children, including yours, thrive when they know the rules and expectations. If you bend the rules or give away your authority, you and your children will suffer the consequences. Most children will show more attention-seeking behavior when those rules are bent or, even worse, when the rules are absent.

This is a very valuable message for parents of a child with special needs. Don't allow your guilt to guide you. Do not feel that you must give in to or protect your children because you perceive that the world has given them an unfair blow. Your children require the same—if not more—structure to define the expectations of their home because there is so much that is unknown in the outside world.

First, you want to establish the hierarchy of your family. It is essential to convey the rules and expectations that you have for each child. If you have very young children, or a child that is a more concrete thinker, establishing a written rule chart as a reminder may be necessary.

You will also want to reinforce the message that you may not always be around to enforce the rules but that when you are not there and someone else is in charge, the rules still apply. By providing this structure for them, your children will have a continued sense of security.

In a household with a child who has special needs, there are many more responsibilities and perhaps fewer experiences in which your children will be overprotected. Rather than feeling uncomfortable with this reality, remember that your home life is the ideal environment for your family to practice for the real world. The more realistic the expectations and demands, the better prepared your children will be to face the challenges and obstacles they are destined to encounter outside your home.

Teach your children the importance of taking responsibility. Convey the significance of having priorities and following through with obligations. Provide concrete examples that reflect the many ways that your focus on completing the tasks associated with your job or with managing the home helps the family. When they complete their responsibilities and have time to "do their own thing," your children will value those opportunities and enjoy them more.

Your role as a parent is not only to provide comfort and security but also to teach your children the value of hard work and the reinforcement that comes with achieving their goals. You want to give your children the opportunity to be children, but at the same time, to acknowledge that everyone has to share the responsibilities of maintaining their home.

There may be times when your children may have to miss a social event or fun outing with their peers to spend time with the family. It is important not to feel that you are burdening them or overwhelming them with responsibility because you are afraid they will resent you or their sibling with special needs. Their active participation in handling their responsibilities within the family is a necessary part of the family dynamic and their personal growth and should be explained as such. Your children should be praised and commended when they maturely accept that duty to family, including when it interferes with time spent with friends.

Whether it is doing age-appropriate chores in the house, completing their homework, or having a part-time job, giving your children the opportunity to accept responsibility and complete a task helps them gain the competence to achieve other more challenging tasks in the future.

Setting Limits

Children need practice to learn appropriate behavior. Teach them to say "Please" and "Thank you" when they are young since it is much more difficult for your children to incorporate these simple behaviors when they get older, if they aren't already part of their routine.

Your children should understand that limits must be set for all of them when they are appropriate. This will help them understand what is expected of them inside and outside of your home.

If you are trying to change a behavior in any child, it is important to be consistent and follow through with the consequences when the inappropriate behavior occurs. A child with special needs or any child seeking attention may test the limits more or may require more practice to eliminate a problem behavior.

This may at times interfere with other family activities and therefore, it is important to balance each child's needs within the family. This situation may require you and you partner to split the group so that one parent can work on addressing a problem behavior while the other parent continues on with a planned family outing. Be sure to communicate with your partner to figure out the best way to keep the family going.

The expectations and the consequences should be clear. After each infraction, take the time to discuss the problem behavior and better choices that your child could make in the future. For example, younger children should learn that running in a store is unsafe, but once the shopping is done, they can run and play at the park. For older children, once a situation is resolved, praise them for their appropriate behaviors or reactions but discuss how they can handle the situation better or differently in the future.

Following Through with Consequences

Remain calm and in control during limit setting. After the consequence, take the time to talk through each situation so that your child will develop the thought process that should precede each action.

Teach your children to develop and ask themselves questions that help them engage in good decision-making behavior. Is this a behavior that will have a positive outcome for them and for others? Are there alternative behaviors they might consider? Might it be more appropriate not to respond?

Children, especially young ones, don't often differentiate between positive and negative attention. They learn that certain behaviors can push their parents buttons and they will often revert to troublesome behaviors whenever it feels right. If you consider the patterns carefully, you will find that there are certain behaviors, such as whining, tantrums, and talking back, which are seen repeatedly. These behaviors may continue and magnify, as your child gets older.

These patterns of problem behaviors presented by both the child with special needs and the siblings should be analyzed to determine whether there are specific circumstances or antecedents that trigger them and whether there are specific consequences that stop them. Once you understand the sequence, you may be able to redirect the behavior before the problem occurs or remind your child of the consequence so the behavior isn't repeated. Through teaching your children to manage their own behavior, you will find that these behaviors become less impactful or diminish entirely.

Other, more benign behaviors, should be ignored completely—this way they will lose their power. For example, though it can grate on your nerves, try not to respond to whining or demanding behavior. If your child has a tantrum, and this includes adolescents, don't respond. Once they have calmed down, have a discussion to help teach your children to put words to their feelings so that they become better equipped at requesting rather than demanding the things they want.

Other behaviors may require an immediate response, especially if they can be damaging or hurtful to the child or others. For these behaviors, such as hitting or cursing, establish a specific consequence, such as time out or taking a privilege away. Use a one or two time warning system and then apply the consequence. Be consistent in your response— consistency in following through with the rewards and consequences for inaction are just as important as learning to complete the tasks. If there are other adults or caregivers who may be interacting with your children, including therapists, relatives and babysitters, ensure that they are aware of the house rules in order to keep the approaches to discipline consistent with each child in your absence.

Children are masters of deception. They can and will try to fool you. Whenever you start to get wishy-washy, your children will sense it and find ways to use it to their advantage.

The consequences for breaking the rules should be suitable for the particular child and appropriate for the behavior demonstrated so that it will motivate a behavior change. This may be challenging with a child whose interests change daily or for a child who may have a tantrum when something important is taken from him.

To eliminate a negative behavior, the response or consequence should be related to the initial behavior and reflect the severity of the wrongdoing. By providing the consequence soon after the negative behavior occurs, the child learns to make a connection between their action and the consequence that occurs. Ideally, you will want to follow through with a brief discussion about the impact of that negative behavior on the child or on others. But it may be difficult to follow through in a timely manner when there is another child in the home who requires immediate attention or when there is an important aspect of the daily routine that cannot be altered. It is as essential for that child—as well as the other children—to provide the one-to-one attention to address their behavior so that all of the children learn that positive behavior has positive consequences and negative behavior has negative consequences.

Caregivers—including grandparents and therapists—and the children should understand the system. Decide in advance whether the other caregivers who may be interacting with your children in your absence will be expected to implement the designated consequences or inform you of the infractions so that you can enforce the consequences. Certain behaviors may require an immediate response and the caregivers should know the expectations. For example, if your child tends to take their seatbelt off while the car is moving, a grandparent must be aware of this behavior and know that they should pull the car over in a safe area until the seat-belt is fastened. If a child cannot travel safely with another caregiver, you may have to make alternate arrangements including getting a babysitter and leaving that child behind.

Be sure that the consequences are appropriate. Some frustrated and overwhelmed parents use an extreme method of punishment and this is not effective. Don't tell your child that you are taking away his toys, that he must go to his room, and that there will be no TV for a week. Though this may be an exaggeration, for a child with frequent misbehavior—and this could include the child with special needs or a sibling who frequently acts out—the extreme consequences received may discourage the child from correcting his or her behavior. Choose a single consequence, prefer-ably something that fits the actions, and stick with it.

Whenever possible, you should try to add rewards and incentives for following the rules. These incentives for good behavior often work just as well as punishments and create more positive energy between you and your child. That child who "forgets" to keep their seatbelt on, may be more inclined to follow the rules if they know there will be a reward for them when they return if Grandpa comes home with a good report.

Figuring out an approach to consequences and rewards that works and feels comfortable for you while finding a way to engage and motivate each child, takes time and mental energy. But once you have figured out a system, you will find that your children will learn to self monitor and will respond more effectively to you, and to their other caregivers, which will make the responsibility of parenting more effortless and tolerable.

Keep in mind that while you may be consistent in your approach, chil-dren are not consistent in their responses. If you were to record your suc-cess with any one technique, you would notice that there are days that the approach works well and other days when it is ineffective.

Even if you periodically experience failure, be resilient and keep try-ing. There is no other responsibility you will face that is as challenging as keeping all of your little ducks in a row. But, as you will learn, there is no other position in life that will be as rewarding when you are successful.

Knowing How and When to Relinquish Control

Parents who seek to control their children often have children who control them and, inevitably, both parent and child feel *more* out of control. Parents who gradually relinquish control have children who cooperate and work with them.

I can remember a friend who would run around the house trying to get her two-year-old son to eat. He was a very fussy eater and every meal was a struggle between them. She would crawl around on the floor as her son played with his toys coercing him to accept each spoonful of food. When the meal (if you want to call it that) was over, she would feel successful knowing that she was able to get some nutrition into her child. But that feeling of success would last for just a few hours until the next mealtime would roll around and they would start the battle over again.

It was obvious to me that the child was controlling his mother. Though it seemed like the most tolerable solution for her at the time, I kept thinking that if she couldn't figure out a way to teach her son to eat independently, she might have to go off to college with him too! The food issue would probably be one of many battles that she would experience with him over time.

Parents who have a child with special needs take note. Here is one moment where you are at an advantage. Because you don't have the luxury of running after any of your children to get them to eat or do anything else, you don't have to worry about all that it will take to undo that behavior.

Children are very perceptive and when given the opportunity they will try to control or manipulate as much of their life as they can. If you give them an indication that they may have the upper hand, they will seize it. And, when they tire of that particular interaction—and they will—they come up with new ways to control you.

I have found that when parents try to control their children's behavior, the children will often act out more when they are outside the home. Many children whose parents allow only healthy foods within their home tend to raid their friend's snack drawers and cabinets whenever they have the chance. If you allow your children to express their individuality, even though you may not always approve, it gives you the opportunity to understand those aspects of their behavior that you do not like and to promote their self-esteem at the same time.

In a sense, the goal is to teach your child the appropriate behaviors in smaller increments and to gradually shape your child's responses. By being a bit less in control, you can actually have a greater impact on your child's behavior than if you tried to control everything that they do.

This is not to suggest that you allow your children to take charge but rather that you avoid creating an autocratic environment. It is ideal to teach your children to understand the expectations so that they learn to control their own behavior.

Your children should be rewarded for trying new things, including foods and behaviors. At the same time, you should try new ways to interact with your children, especially as they mature and old methods are no longer effective.

Keep in mind that you, as a parent, are trying to promote good behavior. As you show flexibility and tolerance toward them, you are teaching your children to do the same toward others. You are showing your children the value of being open-minded and accepting, rather than telling them.

Remember that your primary goal is to act as a director rather than a controller, often pointing out the reactions you and others may have to a given behavior. Guide your child away from those behaviors and activities that may become obstacles for them but do not take those obstacles away because then they will not have the opportunity to learn new, more appropriate behaviors.

You want your children to learn to identify the problems they face and mistakes they have made and to be able to correct them on their own.

Understanding and Coping with Special Needs Behavior

The siblings of a special needs child may be subjected to problematic behavior that is directed at them. They may be hit, punched, kicked or have their hair pulled by their sibling who may have little self-control over their own behavior. It will be important for you to provide your children with the tools to address these behaviors so that they do not respond in angry and aggressive ways or worse, avoid interacting with their siblings.

You should develop ways for your children to deal with these confrontational behaviors. When they are young, you may want them to report disruptive or aggressive behaviors to you so that you can deal directly with the child with special needs. Even a young child could learn to say "No!" in a loud voice when negative behaviors are directed toward them. As they get older, siblings should learn to avoid the triggers that lead to these reactions and to get out of the way to avoid aggression.

You do not want your child to be put in a situation in which they are the disciplinarians; that is your role. They should learn to communicate when they do not appreciate aggressive behaviors that are directed toward them. Similar to the other modeling the siblings will do, this will help the child with special needs learn to control their aggressive behaviors toward other people.

When they are out in public together, certain behaviors exhibited by the sibling with special needs may cause a child to feel embarrassed or angry. Discussing these feelings before they happen will provide your child with the preparation that is necessary to deal with their sibling's acting out behavior.

Keep in mind that your children will be watching your response to these outbursts and that if you remain calm and in control, your other children will learn to do the same.

Disciplining the Special Needs Child

It may be challenging to discipline a child with special needs because you may want to respond with added attention and love, or you may become so frustrated that you respond in anger, yet this may be the child that presents the most challenging behaviors or tests your patience the most. Though some behaviors can be ignored, if you ignore all of them, many will escalate or get out of control. Worst of all, your other children may start to replicate these behaviors to gain attention.

On the other side, your child with special needs may model the behaviors—good and bad—they observe in your other children, but in their own way. For example, a young child with special needs who observes his adolescent sibling yelling at a parent may replicate that behavior with grunts and screams. If that child observes a younger sibling throwing toys, he may throw other objects at his or her peers when frustrated.

It is often challenging to know when a problem behavior is a result of the specific disability or it is a behavior that requires immediate attention. For example, young toddlers may be uncooperative because they lack the language skills to communicate their feelings. They may have a tantrum because they fatigue easily and need a nap. There are many children with special needs that have these same issues, and at times you may want to cut them some slack recognizing that their developmental delay is reflected in many ways beyond their cognitive and language limitations.

Just as you would with your other children, try to give your child with special needs acceptable choices. When engaging in a problem behavior, point out that the behavior is unacceptable and give a warning. Help them put certain words in place to remind them that they are getting close to breaking rules since they may have more difficulty identifying the triggers that lead to problem behavior. When you see that they are on the verge of becoming overwhelmed in a crowded room, ask if they need "break time." For a child with limited communication skills, you may want to establish a signal or gesture, such as holding up their hand, to indicate that it's time for a break.

When your child with special needs misbehaves, make sure that the consequences are clear and immediate. If you find that there are specific triggers to problem behaviors or a particular consequence that is effective with your child, try to convey that information to the other people who are interacting with your child, particularly the siblings, but also your child's teachers, therapists, and babysitters. Providing consistency and following through with consequences is even more important with the child with special needs.

When there is a cognitive delay or a language issue, the child may have difficulty understanding the consequences of his actions and its affect on others. Some children with limited cognitive abilities have difficulty making the connection between behavior and consequences and may require many reminders and coaching in order to make that connection. You may need to reinforce the lesson that running into the street is dangerous by practicing how to reach the edge of the curb without entering the street. If your other children are old enough, have them participate in this practice and/or be role models to teach you child to stop at the edge of the curb.

Convey corrective and instructional information in simple terms that your child can understand. With regard to the consequences, discuss the problem in a manner that your child can comprehend and make sure that the consequences are meaningful to that child.

You will also want to work with your child on self-control. Use certain phrases that are reinforced repeatedly to help control problematic behavior. Simple phrases, such as, "hands to yourself" or "quiet mouth" are terms that your other children can use when they are confronted by an offensive or aggressive behavior.

Handling "Red Flags" and Seeking Intervention When Necessary

In raising children together in a unique household, most of the time, with patience, understanding, rules, and communication, you will be able to correct problem behaviors and conflicts between siblings. There may be times, however, when problems develop that will require more attention and intervention. For example, if a child becomes overly aggressive toward their siblings, you may need the assistance of a behaviorist who could help you put a specific plan in place to address those behaviors in and outside of the home.

In a similar way, if you find that a child exhibits any of the behaviors noted below, you may want to seek counseling from a trained professional:

- Extreme escalation of any behavior
- Problems at school
- Experiences a change in concentration
- Has trouble sleeping or eating
- Exhibits frequent crying
- Shows serious separation anxiety
- Displays signs of withdrawal
- Loses interest in activities

Some children convey their emotional issues through physical symptoms such as headaches or stomach aches. You should first address these concerns with a pediatrician who can help rule out the presence of an underlying physical cause before seeking support from a counselor or therapist. Certainly if there is any discussion about hurting themselves or someone else in a severe manner, you must seek immediate attention or take your child to an emergency room.

In a home with a child with special needs, especially a child with limited communication skills, you may want to consider the fact that this child may be abused or feel abused by a sibling or someone who is responsible for caring for them. Bullying should not be tolerated. Every child must feel safe and that they are protected.

If you see signs of abusive behavior in any of your children, like extreme aggression, physical threats, or verbal assaults, that child may be acting out more severe emotional conflicts and may need to see a trained professional to address the underlying issues. If you are concerned that your child may be abused, either in or outside of your home, trust your instincts and seek assistance from a trained professional.

Giving your child this additional support will demonstrate the seriousness of any extreme behavior and help your child develop more appropriate coping strategies.

Once again, I will reiterate the critical message that as their parents, you should trust your instincts. If you see something that worries you, do not hesitate to find the help your child needs from as many professionals as you think is necessary.

Summary Points
- All children need rules and expectations in order to thrive, but these rules should be specific to their ages and circumstances.
- If rules are broken, it's important to follow through with consequences.
- Determine in advance whether other caregivers will enforce the consequences and be sure to inform both the caregivers and your children of the system that is put in place.
- You should avoid trying to control every aspect of your children's lives, and gradually teach your children to control their own behavior.
- Be more of a director rather than a controller.

- Fostering cooperation and compromise is key to building stronger relationships and alleviating conflict among all your children.
- The child with special needs requires rules too and can often learn positive behavior through example and by modeling from appropriately behaved siblings.
- Teach your children the expected responses to a sibling's misbehavior and encourage them to reinforce positive behaviors as well.
- If you notice any behaviors in any of your children that sends a "red flag" be sure to seek advice from a trained professional.

Chapter 9: Delegating Responsibility and Fostering Independence

Balancing everyone's needs simultaneously is perhaps one of the greatest challenges of managing any family, particularly a diverse set of children.

It is essential to create balance between expecting the siblings to take on responsibilities that are beyond their ability and avoiding placing responsibility on your children because you feel guilty about the fact that they are burdened with the stigma of being a sibling of a child with special needs.

The added pressure and responsibilities may ultimately hinder their ability to become independent and establish an identity outside of the home. At the same time, if you diminish their responsibilities because you feel guilty about their circumstances, it may send a message that you don't think they can handle it. Maintaining balance and discussing the roles they can play will create the best outcome.

Delegating Responsibility

Children need responsibility and learn so much from completing a task from beginning to end. One of the primary ways that children develop self-confidence and self-esteem is by being helpful at home. Giving children household responsibilities helps them feel valued and appreciated for their contribution.

Many busy parents find that it is easier to do things on their own rather than to delegate responsibilities to their children or other people because they don't believe someone else will do the job to their standards. For some, it's a matter of control; for others, its simply a lack of patience—sometimes, it's perceived that it takes less time to undertake a task than explain a task to another. While the latter is probably true, your home is a wonderful training ground for your children who will benefit from each opportunity to practice a new skill. Mastering a variety of tasks will go a long way in increasing their independence and fostering their self-esteem to take on other, more difficult challenges in life.

While trying to keep up with your busy schedule, work, relationships, and running your household, you may feel that the stress increases when you must also manage teaching your children to be responsible. Juggling the many responsibilities of caring for your family and for your home may seem overwhelming, but you will find that as you delegate certain responsibilities to your children, they will become more confident and proficient. As they become more independent and competent, you can entrust them with more responsibility. In the end, everyone benefits.

Practice makes perfect for you and for them. Start with a smaller task like picking out their own clothes, organizing their toys, or putting napkins on the table. A toddler or a child that cannot read could follow a chore chart that has pictures. Initially, it is helpful to have a daily check in to make sure that every step on the chart is completed. Over time though, it should become your child's responsibility to complete the chores and check the chart. This early skill building experience of developing self-reliance and self-competence will go a long way in later years.

The child with special needs should be given tasks that are developmentally appropriate so that he or she can contribute too. Your child can be given the assignment of getting the mail from the mailbox, clearing dishes from the table, or hanging up a coat in the closet. Even though it may not be done correctly every time, be patient and give your child a lot of praise for each attempt to complete the task successfully.

The responsibilities you give your children should increase with the child's age, as should the tasks themselves. Choose small jobs and build on successes. For example, you may find that your child enjoys making pizza or baking cookies. Add pizza night to the weekly menu and gradually delegate more responsibility to your child as he or she masters the skills. The confidence and pride they will gain when people enjoy and compliment their creation will be invaluable.

Choose tasks in which your child shows an interest. At the age of two, a child can be taught to put a spoon next to each plate. By three or four years old, children love to play with water and they enjoy cleaning things. You can combine the two by giving your child the task of cleaning the spoons and unbreakable dishes and sponging down the tables after the meal.

Five and six-year olds can learn to match socks and put them together with a simple twist. They can separate each family member's cleanly laundered clothing into piles so that an older child or adult can fold them and they can help put them away.

School age children can pack their own lunches and help with washing and cutting up vegetables for a salad using a plastic knife. By the age of ten, a child could learn to do the laundry, vacuum, dust, and sweep out the garage.

Try to assign special jobs to each child. Children enjoy doing and sharing creative projects. They can prepare artwork or design bracelets to give each family member as a departing gift at the end of a holiday dinner. Together, the children could create a family collage or calendar on the computer that each family member will receive and enjoy throughout the year. A young child could go through magazines and pick out pictures that depict the favorite activities of each family member, while an older child could embellish the pictures with images from the computer.

Children can work together to create a weekly or weekend calendar so that everyone knows the plans they have, where they have to be, and when. Using markers or the computer your children will enjoy working together to make a project that is original and fun!

You may also want to create a "Family Task Chart." Sometimes the concept of chores has a negative connotation, but using this approach suggests that you are working together as a family to get various jobs done.

There should be an expectation instilled that everyone including the children contributes to the success of the family.

Certain jobs may be expected or required, such as keeping their personal belongings in order, taking care of their hygiene, and other tasks that may earn privileges when they are completed. As children get older, chores and responsibilities usually have to be tied to rewards that are valuable to each child. The time spent in discussing those rewards is a significant part of your establishing a positive relationship with each child and in helping them learn to value the many returns that come from taking on new responsibilities. You will have to balance the rewards so that your child does not become dependent on that reinforcement to get the job done. Frequently reassess the rewards given so that the incentives are appealing and motivating.

Working together with your children on individually delegated tasks will provide yet another opportunity to spend individual time with each child and have quality conversations. It takes a lot of patience and practice to teach your children to tie their shoes and zip their coat, but once they master those skills, they will have them for life. Learning to follow through with a task or chore will go a long way in helping your children gain the independence and competence they will require to complete their assignments at school and at work.

Because you are so busy and involved in juggling so many things at once, you may sometimes forget or neglect the responsibilities that you assigned to each child. If this occurs, try to follow through as soon as you remember.

Becoming Self-Reliant

Raising any child is a daunting task. Parents are given the tremendous opportunity and obligation to turn children into confident, self-sufficient adults who are prepared to live a full and meaningful life. There is an underlying assumption that the more time and energy we put into each child, the healthier and happier they become.

When you are the parent of a family with a child with special needs, there are many obstacles that impede your ability to make each of your children feel that they are the center of your universe. You may even be concerned that you haven't given them enough of your time or attention to succeed on their own. In reality, and for their own sake, none of your children, including the one with special needs, will benefit from having all of your attention.

Given all of the responsibility that you have to care for your family and your home, and likely having to juggle this with a job, too, it becomes essential to teach your children to rely on themselves.

When children grow up in a home with a sibling that consistently requires more of their parents' attention, they learn early on there are other people in their world who need attention and consideration.

Starting at a very young age, the siblings of a child with special needs will learn to be more self-reliant and independent. Whether it is because the child with special needs requires more physical assistance or supervision, the other children will learn that in certain situations, especially when their sibling is unsafe, the parents' focus will immediately turn to the child with special needs. As their parents may frequently get distracted or derailed the other children will develop skills of self-sufficiency that is often beyond their years. You may find that they have to finish dressing themselves, brushing their teeth, or read a book on their own as you are emergently drawn to a child in greater need of your help.

Finding opportunities to encourage your children—even those with special needs—to become as independent as possible is one of the most essential roles as a parent. It will help them to feel proud of themselves and build confidence.

Identify those things that each child can do independently and, during those few quiet moments, help them to learn and practice those skills. Once they have mastered that task, find other skills that they can learn and keep building on their repertoire. The satisfaction they experience each time they learn to do something on their own goes a long way to bolster their confidence for future roles as students, adults, and employees.

Try to find situations where a younger sibling can help an older sibling—it doesn't always have to work the other way around. Keep in mind, that even if that youngster spills the milk when pouring, it is the experience and practice that will help your child master the skill in the future. This concept of "practice makes perfect" applies to the child with special needs as well. As your other children master their skills they can then teach their sibling how to pour the milk and button a coat.

The siblings of a child with special needs may have to demonstrate more patience than other children their age. If you can help them master both the ability to communicate when they need something from you and to delay getting those needs met, even for just a bit, your children will learn vital skills that will help them to function better in the future.

Over time, many children with special needs will develop the skills to be more independent and to occupy themselves. During those quiet moments when your children are able to spend time without you, reading a magazine, doing a puzzle, or playing a video game, take a breath and reflect back on the many times you thought you would never have a minute to yourself.

Promoting Self-Esteem

Children who have high self-esteem believe that they are strong, capable, and worthy of positive experiences, while those with low self-esteem believe that they are inadequate and worthless. Building your child's self esteem is not an easy task but well worth the effort.

Early on, infants learn that their parents will respond to their cries and take care of their needs. Those infants that have attentive parents begin the process of developing a sense of self and well-being. As you continue to express your love and share experiences with your children, their self-esteem is nurtured and they become better able to face life's challenges and setbacks. Children who do not have these early experiences seek validation through other relationships, though they may not really be aware of the feelings that come with that connection.

Helping children to develop self-esteem is even more valuable than your telling your child that you believe in them and what they can accomplish.

You may be hard on yourself feeling that you are not always patient or may not have the time to give each of your children the attention they need. Children are very resilient and it's never too late to start building your child's self-esteem. Each nurturing experience is a building block that creates your child's foundation. Each opportunity to be successful and to be praised for their accomplishments adds more building blocks, which grows and strengthens their development.

Your children's self image will come from the way that they believe others perceive them. Young children, and children with special needs, learn about themselves from their parents' reactions. As they get older, they continue to seek your approval and validation, and they benefit greatly from your statements of pride especially when they aren't expecting them. Take the time to point out what you appreciate in each child and the ways that they have made you proud. Be authentic when providing praise because children can see through a false façade.

Some children may be thin-skinned and may require more security than others. Be aware of each child's needs and provide them with enough reinforcement to get through the most difficult times.

Playtime is a great opportunity for building an intimate relationship with each child, and to give each of them a feeling of importance and accomplishment. When you spend quality one-on-one time playing with your child, you send the message that you value the time you spend together. Let your child select an activity he or she will enjoy. Try to pick a game that will allow your child to be successful but don't throw the game. If you let your child win, you will be sending a message that you don't think he or she can succeed and this may be more detrimental. Don't be too competitive either. It is not about who wins or loses but about the special time that only you and that child will enjoy.

Find a time that the play activity will not be interrupted and you can focus your attention on your child. Make sure that you are there in body and mind, turning off and tuning out other distractions. If your mind is elsewhere, your child will sense that the time together is more of a burden and you will lose out on the opportunity to enjoy all that you can learn from your child.

Some parents struggle with playtime. Consider this an opportunity to invest in your child's self esteem and figure out ways to make your playtime different from their time spent with other family members and friends. Think back to the activities you enjoyed most when you were a child and try to recreate those special times with your child to help them appreciate those activities as well.

Identify each child's talents and give them the opportunity to shine. Whether it is a two-year-old who learns all the words to a song or a six-year-old who masters the steps to a dance, find a place in your home that is the "stage" and give everyone the opportunity to show off their talents. Holiday gatherings are a great time for children to get together, including cousins and family friends, and put on a performance. The time spent working on the "show" will give the adults some time for quiet conversation and the children will benefit from all the applause and attention they get for their efforts.

Teaching your children to explore different interests and to work hard at mastering the skills will go a long way in developing the discipline that is necessary to work hard at school or other tasks that may not come naturally to them.

Monitor teacher and peer influences and the ways that this may have both a positive and negative impact on your children's self esteem. You may not be able to choose your child's teachers or their friends, but you can encourage relationships with people that build your children's character and monitor relationships with those that may be damaging your children's self-worth. Make your home inviting to your children's friends so that you have the opportunity to get to know them. Consider your own relationships with your friends and whether you are modeling relationships in which there is give and take and you are supportive of one another.

Set your children up to succeed and help them get through the failures. If you don't encourage them to try to overcome the roadblocks they face, you will miss out on a great confidence builder. As they work through the challenges and accomplish something they thought was beyond their ability, they will build their confidence far more than through the praise they receive for accomplishing a task that was well within their grasp.

Children value themselves based on how others value them. Be careful not to fall into that trap and avoid comparing them to other people. Don't expect them to excel at everything but encourage them to always try new things. Don't make it about trophies and blue ribbons. By showing that your love is not tied to their accomplishments but rather to the special qualities and characteristics they possess, you children will learn to appreciate those aspects of their personality and to share them with others.

It is Not Always Helpful to be Helpful

Though this may seem counterintuitive, there are times when helping your children may be more detrimental than good. Whether for the child with special needs or your other children, you may feel the need to help your children so that they don't have to struggle. You may feel that they are faced with challenges outside of your home and that it is your responsibility to make things easier for them when they are at home.

In doing so, you are taking away the opportunity to learn how to do the task on their own and gain the much needed independence. You will convey a message that you do not believe your child can accomplish the task and they may give up trying.

You have probably learned this important lesson simply by watching your children take their first steps knowing that they may fall. Chances are you cleared the path for them and helped them up so that they could try again.

As difficult as it may be, it is best to sit back and watch your children grapple with a challenge or task. Whether it is a three-year old who puts his shoes on the wrong feet, the child with special needs who incorrectly buttons a shirt, or a teenager who is struggling with math, if you do the task for your child, you deny him the opportunity to complete it himself and feel pride when the task is successfully completed.

Discuss with your other children the ways in which they can encourage their sibling with special needs to overcome a challenge. For example, they may arrange the shoes with the right shoe on the right side and the left on the left so that the child with special needs can put his shoes on by himself.

Let them be role models and show their sibling how to do the task without doing it for them. I have vivid memories of my daughter practicing the flip-the-coat-over-the-head method for weeks. Even though Jessica eventually learned to put on her coat the regular way, she continued to use the flip method to encourage her brother to master the technique on his own. Once accomplished, she was proud of his achievement and her contribution to his triumph.

Encourage your children to come up with solutions on their own. Show them that approaches that worked in the past can help them to succeed in similar experiences they may encounter. Reinforce the lessons learned and the ways they have grown from each experience.

Have your children share their problems and solutions with each other. You may be quite impressed with what they can teach one another, without parental involvement.

Give your children the opportunity to make mistakes while they are young when the mistakes are much smaller. It is far easier to clean up a spilled glass of juice than to address a serious car accident. Every mistake is a learning experience.

Whether you are dealing with the child with special needs or their sibling, your goal is to provide the encouragement and guidance they need, and let them move forward on their own. If they fall or fail, be there to pick up the pieces and encourage them to try again. As they face each new challenge, be there to help them analyze the experience and figure out how to proceed in a different way next time. Ultimately, your children will build confidence and a solid skill set that will foster independence.

Instilling and Promoting a Sense of Self-Advocacy

When our children were young, I would often take the time to let each of their teachers know that they had a sibling with special needs. Just as parents would inform teachers about their child's individual learning issues or allergies, I felt that it was important to help my children's teachers understand and be sensitive to our home situation. I would ask teachers to let me know if one of my children was struggling since I might be too overwhelmed with other responsibilities to notice a challenge or change.

When our daughter entered middle school, she insisted on speaking to her teachers on her own. She conveyed that although she was certain she wouldn't require any special treatment, she wanted to let her teachers know about her brother's special needs. She developed the courage to share her situation with each teacher.

On another occasion, while shopping for sneakers at a local mall, Jonathan became very unruly knocking shoes off the shelf. Before the situation got out of hand, my husband apologetically explained to the salesperson that our son has special needs and that when he becomes over-stimulated he will act up. There were many times following that incident that I overheard our children using the exact same terms to explain their brother's behavior to friends and strangers.

Our children developed the ability to speak openly about having a sibling with special needs because we set an example for them. That same ability to self-advocate proved helpful when they had to address other issues with teachers, peers, and people in our community.

If your child with special needs has the cognitive and language skills to advocate for themselves help them learn the best approaches to discuss their limitations. You may find that your other children may serve as role models in helping your child with special needs feel comfortable communicating with other people.

Developing Outside Relationships and Interests

Though family time is important, children need time to play with friends without their siblings tagging along. This allows them to develop more age-appropriate social skills and to establish their own identities and personalities. They learn to seek out other children with similar interests and hobbies. Plus, spending time with friends can be fun and be a good distraction for the challenges they may be facing at home.

Friendships provide companionship, and especially in the case of a child whose only sibling has special needs, create an awareness of and appreciation for age-appropriate interaction.

Friendships provide solace and encouragement through difficult times and through times of transition. The support of friends gives children a break from their challenges, as well as peer-based comfort and understanding.

Encouraging your children to develop friendships is a necessity for their emotional and social development. They learn that they must modify their behavior with different people and develop an understanding of other peoples' interests and viewpoints.

Children who have friends have a greater sense of self worth and better self esteem. Through their interaction with friends, children learn the good feeling that comes from having someone by their side and the even better feeling that comes from giving a piece of yourself to someone else who appreciates what you have to offer.

Most children, including those with special needs develop relationships around sharing common interests. Help your children seek out those peers with similar interests through encouraging their involvement in clubs, team sports and after school activities.

Helping Yourself by Helping Others

While growing up in a home with a child with special needs, your children will learn that everyone is different. They learn that despite weaknesses, we are all appreciated and accepted. They learn that we are all given strengths and we must use them each day to make the most of each experience. They learn from their sibling with special needs and from their parents that they must deal with the cards they are dealt.

On a daily basis, our children saw us putting their needs ahead of our own, but they also saw us reaching out to help other people outside of our family who were in need of our support. We have shown them that even when facing misfortune you must not become self-centered or self-focused. Through our participation in community and fund raising activities, our children learned the value of helping others. We immersed our children in an environment that valued the important traits of volunteerism and compassion. Our friends were people who volunteered their time to support other people, and our children looked to them as role models.

Part of fostering independence is encouraging children to apply what they have learned at home to the world outside their home. When they do, they experience great pride in themselves and their accomplishments, as well as the ways in which they touch and positively impact the lives of others.

Learning Life Lessons

Children are accustomed to the experience of learning new lessons through instruction. From a young age, they learn through the words that their parents and teachers impart to them. But the siblings in a special needs family are taught through their parents' actions more than through words. By observing the ways their parents deal with their situation, these children learn to face a challenge with conviction and certainty.

Children with a sibling with special needs learn that there are other people in this world whose needs are important, and at times, more important than their own. They learn that it is valuable and uplifting to do something for someone else. And, if demonstrated and validated by their parents, they grow and develop into unique individuals who can revel in the feeling that they were cherished and appreciated for their actions and contributions.

Living in a home with a child with special needs provides many important life lessons. Parents learn to be patient, positive, and encouraging, regardless of the demands or frustrations. The siblings learn that life is a classroom in which every experience has value and significance. And they may likely demonstrate insight and wisdom well beyond their years.

Perseverance is a personality trait that is inborn, but for the siblings of a child with special needs, it is often a lesson learned through life. As you persevere as parents and face your daily struggles, your children will learn by your example to never give up. The environment that you create will nurture your child's innate qualities and build their self-esteem to face the world with confidence.

Summary Points

- Given the unique challenges special needs families face, delegating responsibility helps keep the balance in the household.
- Teaching self-reliance is a valuable trait to foster in children, especially in those from a special needs family, as they often need to act independently. As they become more independent, children build confidence.
- Spending time with children individually, and discovering and encouraging their unique talents and abilities, helps promote self-esteem.
- Allowing your children to make mistakes or master a new skill on their own will result in a greater sense of accomplishment for them when they succeed.
- Siblings can benefit from learning how to advocate for themselves and their siblings. Self-advocacy builds character, and helps other people that they encounter become more knowledgeable and enlightened.
- Children need to establish relationships and build friendships outside the home to become more well-rounded.
- Siblings of a child with special needs are naturally more empathetic and often grow up to become more compassionate and tolerant.

Part IV: Life Outside the Home

Chapter 10: Facing the World Together

People tend to draw conclusions about the experiences of the siblings in a special needs family that are often based on their belief of how difficult the experience might be for them. They see our children as more vulnerable or burdened and feel sorry for them.

Our children sense this when they interact with people and it makes them feel uncomfortable and apprehensive. In addition, many people are concerned that they may do or say something that may be hurtful to the siblings. They tend to withdraw from them rather than provide the comfort and support they need. These experiences cause the siblings to feel more vulnerable and unsure.

Parents should play an active role to ensure that their children are treated fairly and respectfully. Whether your children are interacting with friends or strangers, you should be vigilant and intervene when necessary.

Though some children may put on a brave face, they are often vulnerable to the impact of other peoples' negative perceptions of them. Teach your children to identify their feelings about being judged or misperceived, and help them articulate the need for support.

The Cost of Shame

After presenting at a conference, I was approached by a young woman who asked to speak with me privately. She told me that she thought she might have a brother with special needs who had been sent to live in an institution at birth. She never met the brother but heard her parents discussing him in private conversations. After hearing my presentation about sibling relationships in a special needs family, she wondered whether I thought she could ask her parents about her brother.

I have worked with several families that are very guarded and don't share information about life at home. Many parents discourage—even forbid—their children to talk to outsiders about their sibling with special needs. Some even prohibit discussions at home. These children are often burdened with the responsibility of harboring the family's secret. They are fraught with distress that they may hurt their sibling if they discuss the situation with friends, extended family members, teachers—or even their own parents.

These children are taught to believe that there is a tremendous stigma associated with having a sibling with special needs and they become consumed with the shame and embarrassment that goes with having a member of their family that is "different." Whether the child with special needs lives in the home or at another location, in most instances, the feelings of shame stem from the parents who rarely discuss their situation.

In speaking with siblings, over the years, I have found that these children experience a great deal of anxiety and are concerned that if they share information about their sibling's special needs, something bad will happen to their family or they will hurt their parents.

One of the saddest situations I encountered was meeting a seventeen-year-old girl whose older sister with special needs lived in the home but her parents were so secretive they did not share their experiences. This young girl was ashamed to tell her friends that she had a sister with special needs and would not—could not—invite anyone to her house. As she got older, it became more difficult to introduce a sibling that no one had ever heard about or met, so she continued to keep her sister's existence a secret. As it turned out, several friends in the neighborhood knew about the sister but never mentioned it to this girl because she had not shared her situation with them.

Imagine the pressure this young girl felt every time she and her friends were trying to make plans. When discussing what they would do or where they would go after school or on the weekend, this girl would avoid inviting friends to or near her house. No doubt, her focus was not on the activity or opportunity to socialize, but rather, to make sure that the plans would take her far away from her home.

As such, she never had the opportunity to host a sleepover or spend time with friends hanging out in her room or basement, playing games, listening to music, or gossiping about a cute boy. She couldn't even invite classmates over from school to do homework together or work on a group project.

Because her family was so secretive, the sibling with special needs was deprived of opportunities to meet new people or develop social skills. In fact, the entire family was denied the opportunity to develop relationships with other people who may have been supportive and had a positive impact in their lives.

Even though we have made great progress in acceptance of those with disabilities, you may be part of a family that still feels shame or discomfort about a child who is different. While you may find your child to be manageable at home, once you are out in public, your child may act in ways that make it very uncomfortable for you or your children. Despite the progress, you may still have to deal with the judgment or opinions of others (or the concern of how others will observe you or your children interacting with the child with special needs).

Some family members may cope better than others. It is normal and understandable for you and your children to feel shame or embarrassment at times. But measures can be taken to dispel the shame, as there is nothing to feel bad about. Other people do not define you, your family, or your children, or even a child with special needs. You each define yourself. While others may perceive your family as unusual, it's important for you to convey to others that you are a special family with a special child.

Rather than run from the situation, I have learned that it is often best to explain it to observers. You may find that they are eager to share their own experiences about their family members who have special needs or about those family members who are "just special."

Opening Your Home

Though it was never easy, especially when our son was young and his behavior more erratic, we always had an open door policy in our home. Even though there were times when he would act out if visitors ignored him, our children's friends were invited to our home and their brother often became part of the group.

There were many times that Jonathan would try to get attention through his misbehavior, but over time, our children's friends learned to deal with his differences and he learned to be less intrusive. There were embarrassing moments and times when he would yell or curse, but we still included Jonathan in activities and our guests, even young children, learned to interact with him.

Initially, when he was a cute baby or a fun toddler, our older children's friends enjoyed playing with him. As he got older, they adapted to his differences. There were times, especially when we moved, that our children worried about how their new friends would react. Our daughter's friends were more inquisitive and not shy about asking questions, and as they gradually got to know more about Jonathan, they would invite him into their circle. Our sons' friends were less curious. They just hung out with Jonathan and included him in their games.

We never insisted that our children and their friends include Jonathan in their activities and because we let them have time alone with their friends, our children and their friends began to include Jonathan once they were prepared to accommodate his differences. When a large group was invited over to the house, we would often assign a friend or family member to be with Jonathan so that if he needed to separate from the group they could accompany him. At other times, we would plan an outing alone with Jonathan so that the crowd wouldn't overwhelm him and he wouldn't interfere with the group's activities. Other times, we would plan activities for the group that would include him.

For example, early on Jonathan learned to shoot a basketball. The group of boys would play basketball and Jonathan would play along. Since he was an excellent swimmer, there were many times that the group would all swim together, and although he wasn't always included in their games, Jonathan felt included.

Not everyone welcomed him with open arms, but as long as we let the group decide if or when to include Jonathan, the children were more willing to do so. And by opening our home to others, Jonathan learned to interact with many different people and they, in turn, learned something from him.

It is important to begin discussing the situation openly when your children are younger. For example, we used the phrase "different" when discussing how everyone has various strengths and weaknesses. We emphasized that he was very social and enjoyed being around people, even if he couldn't always let them know it.

I can recall one afternoon when my daughter and her four-year old classmates were sitting in the backseat of my car. One of the little girls asked me why our son would scream when he wanted something. After explaining developmental delay to these girls in terms they could understand, I asked each of them to identify a way in which they were different from their friends. One girl spoke about her curly blonde hair and the second one mentioned that she had a very deep voice.

Once we acknowledged our differences, I explained that people express themselves in different ways. I asked the girls to convey something they wanted through pantomime. It took a while for them to get their messages across and they giggled as they got through the exercise. But it taught them a valuable lesson about different methods of communication.

This activity also helped the girls to see how fortunate they were to be able to use words to convey their needs and wishes and how there may be times when people with special needs cannot express something important to those around them.

As a result, the girls developed a clearer understanding of Jonathan's situation and perhaps more empathy toward him and our daughter.

Anyone can learn valuable lessons from similar exercises and through the inclusion of individuals with special needs into their community and home. By opening your home to others, you can enlighten them to your family's experiences, challenging and triumphant. The more we expose others to people with differences, the more those differences dissipate.

The Influence of Extended Family

Even in close, supportive families, there are many extended family members—grandparents, aunts, uncles, or cousins—that may not be open-minded, tolerant, or supportive. Some family members may be neutral and others may feel awkward. Many relatives may want to be more connected but may not know how to do or say the right thing.

We were very fortunate and I recognize that our circumstances were somewhat unique. Many of our siblings are in the fields of medicine and education, so that made them uniquely qualified to become the aunts and uncles of a child with special needs. Our children's childhood was influenced by the tremendous support that we received from our family who made themselves available to help us care for all of our children. This gift had resounding effects that are immeasurable.

As my children saw their aunts and uncles spending time with Jonathan—interacting, talking, singing, and playing with him—they learned new and better ways to interact with him. The most unexpected outcome was that our nieces and nephews engaged in similar activities and learned to accept their cousin.

Rather than instructing their children to "be nice to Jonathan because he was special," our brothers and sisters showed their children that they appreciated and loved our son. These interactions were also beneficial to our children who saw their brother's value through other people's eyes.

As adults, our nieces and nephews have become involved in activities and special needs programs, which were, no doubt, directly influenced by the experiences and interactions they had with our family.

It is very valuable to engage your extended family early on so that they can gradually develop a level of comfort over time. In most families, there is usually a child (or two) without special needs that can be annoying or more demanding, yet families seem to learn to tolerate or work around that child.

Encourage your extended family to engage in activities that your child with special needs enjoys, whether it is listening to music, watching videos, or drawing. Plan activities that will allow all of the children—yours along with your nieces and nephews—to play together, and when necessary pair up one of the more mature and tolerant cousins with the child with special needs so that they can help him or her interact.

Conversely, you may find that there are relatives who mean well, but become overbearing and annoying, especially when they call to give you advice without fully understanding your child's situation—they wind up discussing another type of disability or other issues that do not apply to your child. When confronted with this situation, just listen, nod politely, but then do what you know is best. There is little benefit in trying to help them understand your unique circumstances and nothing to be gained from hurting their feelings or distancing them.

Dealing with Ignorance

You are probably already aware that there are many ignorant people in this world and that not everyone is able to appreciate a child with special needs—or even your other children—as you do. There are many circumstances in which peers, or a narrow-minded adult, ridicules or mistreats the sibling of a child with special needs. I have encountered many situations in which misinformed parents do not allow their children to play at the homes of children with a sibling with special needs. Further, the news frequently reports disturbing circumstances in which an aide assigned to assist a child with special needs winds up neglecting or bullying the child. Fortunately, we are more aware and far less tolerant of these types of biases and, in most cases, these prejudiced individuals are facing consequences for their actions.

Unfortunately, you may still find that there are bullies all over and that bullies come in all sizes. It's not limited to children—many adults act aggressively, and your children should know that this behavior is unacceptable.

The bullying may be directed at your child with special needs, your other children, and at you. When the bullying is directed at any of your children, it is natural for you to become exceedingly protective and irate—like a protective mother or father bear. Take a moment to assess the circumstances before reacting and when necessary find the support you need to right the wrong.

Identifying bullying may be difficult because some bullies are subtle, but if you find verbal or non-verbal behavior that makes you feel uncomfortable it is likely a sign of bullying. Help your child learn to identify bullying and let them know that they should communicate with you when they feel that others are acting that way toward them.

If you find that your child is experiencing a change in sleep patterns, mood, or avoids school or afterschool activities, you may want to ask whether someone is bothering or picking on them.

If the bullying is occurring at school, speak with a counselor or principal and address your child's rights to be protected. Provide detailed information and encourage your child to communicate any confrontations.

If the bullying is occurring in a playground or during an afterschool activity, speak with the offending child's parents or other authority figures that may be able to address the issue with the child. It is best not to confront the child directly because in doing so, you may be perceived as a bully. However, if there are no other options readily available I don't discourage this approach completely. In doing so, speak specifically about the troubling behavior and not about the child. Avoid calling the child a bully, but rather let him or her know that it is hurtful and unacceptable to act rudely or aggressively to other people.

Help your children to rally their friends for support. Children are less likely to bully another child when others are around and your child will have more strength to avoid the bully when others are there for them.

If any of your children experiences physical harm or severe harassment you should intervene with the proper authorities. If you find that the school is not cooperative, you may want to consult with an attorney or contact the police. These circumstances are very serious and should not be tolerated. Your children should know that they have rights and you are there to protect them.

This advice also applies when the bullying is directed at you. Remain calm and assess the situation before determining your plan of action to confront the individual who is bullying you. You may choose to speak with them immediately and directly or else find another, more opportune time to address the situation. Stay focused on the bully's behavior and let them know that it should cease.

Your focus should be on educating ignorant people rather than confronting them. When faced with individuals that cannot or will not be educated, protect yourself and your family, and then move on.

Hopefully, as we immerse our children into the community and provide more opportunities for other people to appreciate them, the world will become a more tolerant place for everyone with differences.

Building a Community

Once you have established your rhythm as a family and have helped your children to identify who they are both in and outside of your home, you will find that you are better prepared to face the world. You will have established a parenting style that works well with your children and they will know your expectations of them. You will be able to face new challenges together and your children will be prepared to face the world on their own.

There are many incredible resources for special needs families, many of which start in your own community, so you should explore and take advantage of these programs and opportunities.

The School Experience

All of our children were extremely fortunate to attend a mainstream school with a self-contained, special education classroom program that allowed Jonathan to attend school with his siblings. In this unique environment that included grades Pre-K through high school in the same building, all of the students at the school learned tolerance. The older children learned to accept younger children and the mainstream students learned to appreciate the children with special needs. Our children rode the same bus to school, shared a cafeteria, and interacted with each other throughout the day. All of the children were included in afterschool activities and sports teams. This provided the remarkable opportunity for our children and their friends to be a part of their brother's life and he in theirs.

Their school environment nurtured acceptance and inclusion. The children with special needs were mainstreamed with their typical classmates in various activities throughout the day and the children in the regular education school were invited into the special education classroom for various programs and opportunities.

The amount of change that occurred in all of the children in that school went well beyond anything that could be recorded on a report card. Rather than developing prejudices and fears about children with special needs, these young children learned to interact with and include them in their activities.

Though the educational benefits are not always evident, the inclusion of special education children with typically developing children has far reaching effects that go way beyond bridging the gap between the education offered to children in regular education and those in special education. The positive outcome is a greater acceptance of people with special needs and their introduction into the mainstream community.

Tolerance isn't learned through a lecture; it is best learned through interaction. Through these programs that encourage inclusion, all children feel that they are making a meaningful contribution to the life of their peers. Even at a young age, they feel empowered by having other children follow them, appreciate their interactions, and emulate their behavior. In this situation, the siblings take on special roles, showing their friends and classmates the best ways to interact with their sibling with special needs.

The child with special needs learns a great deal from his relationships with his siblings and their peers. He learns many positive behaviors and has the opportunity to receive both positive and negative feedback regarding his own behavior. This experience teaches self-awareness and helps the child with special needs gain self-esteem and the camaraderie of others.

While there is some debate about the value and limitations of inclusion programs, based on real life research, there are strong indications that early and regular interaction with individuals who are different will have a positive impact on most children.

Over the years, I have seen many new and innovative programs developed based on this premise and this trend will continue if you and other like-minded parents become advocates for these programs.

The Internet is a rich resource for many of these remarkable programs, and as mentioned, other special needs families especially those with older children who have walked in your shoes can often offer invaluable information.

Working with Teachers

Teachers are critical and influential mentors and role models to children throughout their academic years. Since my children attended a private school, I had the opportunity to develop a relationship with many of their teachers and found that they were often eager to help all of my children. Teachers should be made aware of your children's unique family situation and the manner in which they can be helped. If a teacher is cautious when interacting with your child because he or she knows there is a sibling with special needs at home, explain that your child should have the same goals and responsibilities as the other students in the class.

You may encounter a teacher who avoids assigning a family project because he or she is concerned that it might be uncomfortable for your child. Help that teacher understand that your child is just as proud of each of their siblings as any other child in the class. Your children should be encouraged to do a family project, particularly one in which they can showcase each family member's best traits and strengths.

This is not to suggest that you need to become overly involved in the teacher/child relationship, but rather that you should feel comfortable in providing guidance that will foster that relationship. Given your familiarity with your children's likes and dislikes, you can be a trusted and informed resource to teachers and someone with whom they should feel comfortable communicating.

You should also feel comfortable checking with and even correcting a teacher when you think he or she may have overlooked something important. If something troubles you, chances are there is a reason and you should communicate your concerns.

Many teachers are eager to help and can be another resource for your child. Teachers should be encouraged to ask your child questions about their sibling with special needs so that they are better equipped to intervene and provide your child with support at school.

For example, a teacher might hear your child mention that her sibling with special needs interferes with her life. The teacher could, in turn, point out that all siblings have that experience at times and that she is available to listen to and support in any way that she can.

Ordinarily, family life doesn't enter the classroom, but you may encounter a teacher who is less sensitive or understanding. If this occurs, empower your child to advocate for himself or arrange for a parent/ teacher conference so that you can educate the educator. Depending on the circumstances, you may want to discuss the matter with the school's guidance counselor or principal.

Community Programs

We were part of a remarkable community in which many worthwhile programs existed or evolved over time. Many of these programs were developed as a result of the special needs families in the community joining together to fill a void. Several of these programs were started to provide respite for the families with a child with special needs but grew to include support to the siblings, parents, and extended families. Over time, those who volunteered to work with the children with special needs and their families derived great benefit, and these individuals became active in advocating for more inclusive programs.

Years ago, I was involved in the development of the "Friendship Circle," a program that helped foster relationships between teen volunteers and children with special needs. Through this program, the teens would visit the children with special needs and interact with them in their homes. Initially, the program involved ten teens and five children with special needs. Over the years, the program in our community has grown to include over eight hundred teen volunteers and three hundred children with special needs; and the program is now available in many other communities throughout the country.

As the parents and the volunteers came forward with suggestions, the program grew from having teens volunteer for weekly home visit to the development of holiday and Sunday morning programs. When parents requested help with finding activities for their children during school vacations, summer and winter camp programs were started. This program expanded to include outings for parents, support groups for grandparents, and special events for siblings.

Several years later, sports teams were developed so that the children with special needs could learn karate, baseball, and basketball.

The Friendship Circle created a "Friends in the Community Program," in which volunteers were recruited to accompany teens with special needs on outings to the movies, grocery store, bank, and shopping mall. As time passed and the children grew older, the latest innovative program is a monthly social for adults with special needs that include many of the same volunteers who are now adults and are attending college.

Interactive programs like these are far more beneficial than typical support groups. They provide opportunities for the children with special needs to engage in typical, age-appropriate activities. Concurrently, parents have the opportunity to connect, socialize, and exchange information with each other. One of the greatest benefits is that the other children can participate in or take pride in watching their sibling with special needs learn new skills, socialize with peers, and be a part of a team.

In addition, programs were developed for grandparents, aunts, and uncles so that they could spend time with and interact with the child through trips or other activities. Through these programs, they met other extended family members of special needs families, and have formed their own unique bonds.

There are many programs like this all over the country. If these programs already exist in your community, consider getting involved because the benefits are far-reaching. If these programs are not offered in your community, you may want to reach out to a religious group or special needs organization to spearhead the programs on your own or with other special needs families.

You can seek out programs that include and mainstream children with special needs into afterschool and summer programs. Through your local community, school district, religious organization, or through family events, you can create inclusive experiences that are very valuable for all your children and those with whom they socialize.

In today's world, there's no reason why any member of a special needs family should have to hide their child or their feelings away.

Summary Points
- The siblings of a child with special needs may be perceived or treated differently than other children and parents need to be mindful and vigilant to outside influences or responses.
- While it's not unnatural for some families to feel a sense of discomfort when including their child with special needs, it's healthier for everyone to break the pattern by enlightening others to be open-minded.
- When possible, encourage your children to bring friends to the house and be honest about your child's differences to dispel negative perceptions and assumptions, and instead, encourage compassion, understanding, and inclusion.

- Similarly, enlighten and include extended family members to visit and to share in your children's accomplishments.
- Strive to develop a relationship with your children's teachers since they will provide insight to how your children are coping outside of the home. Help them overcome any misconceptions about a special needs family.
- When people come from a place of ignorance, they often behave toward you, your family, and your child with special needs in negative ways, so whenever possible, work to inform and correct negative assumptions.
- If any of your children is the victim of bullying in any way, take measures to rectify the situation by informing parents, school administrators, or if need be, confront and point out the hurtful behavior in a calm and intelligent manner.
- Initiate or participate in school programs that foster acceptance and/or inclusion. These types of programs can benefit all children and build understanding and personal growth.
- Seek out and join forces with other special needs parents and families in your area for support. Join together to develop local programs and resources that will support your children and your family.

Chapter 11: Creative Solutions
for Everyday Encounters

Being creative and well prepared will help everyone get through the most challenging events. You will learn from each experience and be better prepared the next time something similar rolls around.

You will find that if you have the materials available to you, you can get out of any "sticky situation." Just as a mother of an infant keeps her bag at the door, if you are prepared for the inevitable melt down, either your own or your child's, you will feel more confident as a parent and things will go more smoothly.

Create and Carry a "Going Out Bag"

I may have felt like Mary Poppins at times, but I never left home without a bag that was filled with all of the supplies to occupy my children. As they got older, my children each had their own backpack in the front hall closet that was filled with the individual items that they each enjoyed, and we were always prepared to leave the house at a moment's notice. Having these bags ready to take on the go alleviated a lot of stress for everyone, especially when we were dealing with an emergency situation.

If I wanted to attend and enjoy one child's sporting event, I would have to keep my other children entertained. If my child with special needs came too, he would require many different activities to get through a quarter. Those going out bags proved to be a lifesaver.

Each of the individualized and age-appropriate activities will keep your children entertained when you take your family to restaurants, the mall, or to a family dinner. You will find that when your child is entertained, you can focus on the road during a long car trip or deal with a doctor in a hospital emergency room. These personalized activities can help to avoid stressful moments and make any family outing more enjoyable.

Though many children are using hand-held devices, such as smart phones and video games, as their entertainment, there may be certain circumstances and environments that are not conducive to these activities, and these other supplies may come in handy. The items you can stock in the bag will vary from child to child, depending on age and gender.

Here are some ideas for creating your child's personalized bag:

- A waterproof bag or backpack that is unique for each child (in a favorite color or superhero or Disney character, etc.) should be designated just for "going out"
- Juice box/bottled water/sports drink
- Mini bottle of hand sanitizer
- Pack of tissues
- Book, comic book, magazine
- Small electronic or travel version of board game
- Deck of cards
- Crayons/markers
- Workbook, crossword puzzles, word searches, etc.
- Coloring book
- Action figures, Barbie doll, or car collection
- Legos or blocks
- Small puzzles or games

Ideally, these items should be kept in the bag, and ready to go at any time. If each child has his or her own supplies and these supplies are only used when you are out of the house, the items will be cherished and your child will look forward to the activities.

Holiday Dinners and Visits with Extended Family

Holidays are supposed to be happy occasions when families reconnect, enjoy a festive meal together, watch a football game, or play in the backyard. But even in closely-knit families, tensions could arise due to clashes of personality, whiny or restless children, or impatient older relatives. Here too, you will find that preplanning goes a long way in maintaining a safe and positive experience for everyone.

Whether hosting a gathering in your own home or visiting someone else's home, start by finding out which family members will be in attendance and how knowledgeable, understanding, and accommodating these relatives will be to your family circumstances. This way, you will know in advance what to expect and how best to prepare for your encounters with them.

When you are expecting out of town relatives or other houseguests who will be staying at your home overnight or for several days, it is often stressful to clean and cook for your guests, but also disruptive to the schedules and structure you have in place. Discuss the changes that will take place with the child with special needs, and with your other children, so that they will know what to expect before your guests' arrival. If your child has difficulty sharing favorite possessions, put those items in a special place until the guests have left. If your visitors are planning an extended stay, you may want to suggest and plan outings they can do on their own so that you and your children have a chance to be alone in your own home for a few hours.

If you know that certain relatives are disorganized or have small children that plow through your children's belongings or toy chests, you may want to put away all of the large puzzles or large buckets of Legos, so you are not left sorting them all out for hours after your guests leave. If your family members have time-management issues, try to plan a menu that will allow you to keep the meal flowing in case there are late arrivals. And prior to their arrival, rehearse a self-soothing statement of "their visit is time limited and we will get through it."

When you know that there will be many children in the house with different abilities and personalities, try to plan activities that promote co-operative rather than competitive play. Encourage the children to work together on a large mural that depicts the holiday theme, or to work on a talent show that the adults will view after dessert.

If you find that a relative is intolerant or insensitive to your family situation, be sure to address it with them either before their arrival or soon after to avoid any misunderstanding. Offer suggestions on ways they could adapt their behavior to better adjust to your child with special needs. One of the benefits of a large family dinner table is that seats can be assigned based on tolerance and the grumpy aunt or uncle can be placed at the other end of the table. Better yet, having a designated children's table or a separate section at the main table allows the children to come and go based on their attention span, and helps keep the conversation flowing at the adult table.

Don't feel judged by family members that may not understand or accept your child with special needs or how you manage them. It is their issue and not yours. If you feel confident in your decisions—and you should—it will be easier to smile and ignore any unflattering comments or unsolicited advice.

If you are visiting someone's home for a day or longer, come prepared. Not every relative has the space, accouterments, or understanding to create a welcoming and comfortable environment for your family. Bring along everyone's "going out" bags and any specific items you will need to accommodate your child with special needs. Make use of the car ride or other travel time to talk about what to expect at your destination in terms of who will be there, what to anticipate, and how to behave. Establish a way in which any of your children can privately express to you any problems or discomfort they are feeling so that you can be helpful and get their needs met.

Family Outings

It is important to schedule family activities on a regular basis. This may require a great deal of creativity and flexibility, but you will find many activities that everyone can enjoy. In our family, regular outings for ice cream and family vacations were a great opportunity for everyone to bond and share good times together. My grown children still refer back to these experiences with nostalgia and positive feelings.

Family outings should encourage positive interaction on many different levels of ability to accommodate your children's varying physical and cognitive skills. Our family enjoyed swimming, basketball, ice-skating, and bowling. Each family member would engage in the activity at their individual level and there were many opportunities for teaching new skills and commending accomplishments.

There may be times when your children feel that their sibling with special needs is holding them back. Be prepared to come up with a creative solution. You may want to bring a relative, friend, or babysitter to spend time with your child with special needs so that you can spend time interacting with your other children.

For example, family outings to the movies may require some flexibility if your children are different ages or have different interests. We often had to split up at the multiplex, with each parent going to a different movie with one or two of the children. We chose similar show times so that we could all travel together in the car. After the movie, we would all go out for ice cream and share the details about the movies we saw.

As children with special needs often lack boundaries or patience, it can be a challenge to keep the child from eventually being disruptive, so it takes some creativity to find a workable solution. When planning a dinner at a restaurant, for example, we often traveled in two cars so that half of the group could be seated and the food would be ordered before Jonathan arrived. In certain restaurants that we frequented, we often ordered our food over the phone in advance so that it could be served as soon as we arrived and we could eat together as a family. The restaurant owners were surprisingly willing and eager to comply because they appreciated that this method helped us to avoid disturbing the other patrons.

Another creative solution for restaurant outings is to create a family night out at a local restaurant with other special needs families. Work with the restaurant manager in advance to find a designated location in the restaurant for all of the families in your group. This way, if some of the children are noisy or get up to walk around they won't disturb the other patrons. This type of event creates a more tolerant environment and gives siblings and parents the chance to get together as well.

Special Needs-Friendly Vacations

Family vacations may be a bit more challenging when you are including a child with different needs but you should not avoid planning them, since these trips create strong family bonds and are extremely important for every family member.

Preparing for a Vacation

If your vacation entails a long car trip, be sure to discuss your expectations for the time spent in the car. Before leaving the house, you should rehearse the rules repeatedly with your children. For some children, providing a written rule chart may be helpful.

Let your children know that they must remain in their car seat or keep their seatbelt fastened at all times and that only quiet voices can be used inside the car. Plan activities that will keep all of the children engaged while on the road. Be prepared to stop every hour or two, depending on the age and attention of the children, for bathroom breaks and to give the children the opportunity to stretch and run around. Emphasize that while you would encourage your children to interact and have fun, everyone must keep their hands to themselves at all times and verbal outbursts will not be tolerated. There are many car ride games or travel versions of board games that can be purchased. Portable devices can be borrowed or bought, so that your children can watch their favorite videos. You may want to set the schedule as if the children are viewing movies at a theatre before you leave to avoid conflict during the trip.

Since this is a special experience and you may be spending a considerable amount of money, you may find that spending a bit more will enhance the experience for everyone involved, including other families you encounter. We often paid someone to travel with us or arranged to have a sitter or aide join us at the destination to serve as Jonathan's chaperone. If you cannot afford or find a babysitter, you may be able to find a high school or college student, a friend's teenager, or a responsible niece or nephew that is eager to go on an all-expenses paid vacation without getting any additional salary. You might be able to find a Big Brother/Sister for your family by adopting a teenage neighbor who is either an only child or the youngest in a family and eager to join a big family vacation.

Whether it is a Big Brother/Sister, babysitter or shadow that person should be capable of spending time with the child with special needs, either alone or with your other children, so that you can alternate between time spent with each child, time with groups of children, and time alone with your spouse. Your child with special needs will enjoy the outings more when they have a designated person available to accommodate their needs, whether it is taking a break or choosing a slower ride, and the vacation experience will be more enjoyable for everyone be-cause that child can go at his or her own pace.

Certainly if your child requires that level of supervision in a self-contained classroom it is unfair to expect him or her to behave any differently when in an unfamiliar surroundings with many more distractions. Further, since it may be rare or costly to get away together as a family, you will want to do whatever you can to minimize your stress and create a memorable time for everyone.

Upon Arrival

Hotels are now more accommodating and offer many ser-vices to special needs families.

Wherever we traveled, we would get adjoining rooms in a hotel or find a hotel room with a small kitchen area and family space. These accommodations would provide more opportu-nities for the family to be together and provide an area for any family member to separate from the group for alone time when needed. We would often prepare light meals in the kitchen and save restaurant time for meals when everyone was adequately rested and able to handle the extra stimulation. Many hotels will provide refrigerators and other items by request, particularly if you call and ask for them in advance.

We would try to find a separate area of the hotel's pool or swim at an off peak time so that our children would not disturb the other swimmers. When the pool or play area was too crowd-ed, our family enjoyed long walks together to explore our new environment.

Though we may have felt a bit uncomfortable at first, we finally took advantage of the special needs pass at the Disney resorts that allowed our family priority access to some of the attractions. Many other theme parks, zoos, and museums have similar accommodations that provide special privileges for children with special needs and their families, and this information can be obtained online or at guest services.

Many ski resorts have tandem skiing to allow an instructor or family member to ski together with a person with special needs. If you choose to stay local, there are wonderful attractions including apple picking, horseback riding, and children's museums that have accommodations for a family member with special needs.

Resources:

There are numerous organizations and websites that provide information about traveling with special needs children. More and more information becomes available each year but here are some places to start:

- Family Vacation Critic: http://www.familyvacationcritic. com/special-needs-travel/art/
- Transportation Security Administration: http://www. tsa.gov/traveler-information/children-disabilities
- Friendship Circle: http://www.friendshipcircle.org/ blog/2012/06/06/32-vacation-destinations-for-individuals-with-disabilities-or-special-needs/

Finding Extra Help Outside of the Family

One of my most creative solutions in raising a large family that included a child with special needs is a concept that I have termed, "care share."

During the many hours that my husband was at work, I had extra hands available so that each child would have more attention. Sometimes in lieu of vacations and big family outings, extra money went toward hiring childcare during the day or after school.

I often hired a babysitter that was a college student or retiree and had a car. Our babysitter would take the younger two for a walk in their stroller while I did homework with the older two, or take the older two children out to their piano lessons while I gave the younger ones a bath and got them ready for bed. The babysitter could drive Jonathan to his therapy sessions while I attended a Little League game with our sons.

If you can't afford the extra babysitter, I would recommend trying to find an older person or a teen in your neighborhood that might be available to volunteer to help. Many high school and college students have requirements for community service and would enjoy working with young children. Graduate school programs are a resource for individuals who are planning a career in education, counseling or a health related field and may be willing to gain experience through spending time with your family. Perhaps you have older neighbors whose children and grandchildren don't live nearby. They might enjoy helping out by spending time with your children, including the child with special needs. If you find the right person, he or she could become part of your extended family and over time they will appreciate the love and care your children give them in return.

Other Creative Solutions

One of my best suggestions that I have given many parents including those with children with special needs comes from my experiences with our son who as a toddler seemed to require very little sleep. When he was two and a half years old and was sharing a room with his older brother and our live-in babysitter, his sleep patterns and frequent middle of the night awakenings became a tremendous issue for everyone in the household. Out of desperation, and the need to be able to get up in the morning to go to work, I came up with a great solution.

Each night, we would walk around the house and select three special activities that he would be eager to do during that night. Before we went to bed, I would set up each activity in front of one of the chairs of the child-sized table I kept in the room, and in front of the fourth chair, I would put a snack. During his middle of the night awakening, instead of waking up a family member for companionship, he would color, play with Play-Doh, do puzzles, string a necklace out of Cheerios, and read books quietly on his own. I tried to select activities that would keep his attention but that weren't too stimulating so that he would eventually go back to bed. He would eagerly anticipate the broad range of activities that were left for him to complete and we would relish the extra sleep.

In addition, I purchased a child's alarm clock that played his favorite song when it went off. He learned that when he would get up at night he could play in his room but that he could not come out of his room until the alarm went off in the morning. Although I am convinced that at times he would wake himself up to play, it really didn't matter because he didn't wake anyone else up. Eventually he learned to sleep through the night and we all survived the extended "terrible twos"—including him!

Years later, when Jonathan could not sit at the dinner table, and was especially uncomfortable during large family gatherings, I selected a few drawers in our room where we kept his "Special Activities." He would leave the table, and go up to our room where he would entertain himself. At times, he enjoyed those special activities so much that it would be difficult to persuade him to come downstairs to say goodbye to the guests.

These examples illuminate the phrase that "necessity is the mother of invention." The ideas you devise to help any of your children get through a difficult stage will go a long way in helping the entire family to thrive.

Family Bonding Time

When my children were young, I would play with them while exercising. I took turns holding each of them up in the air with my legs (an excellent exercise for postpartum abs) and we would all have fun with each other. We did not require any high-tech equipment and we didn't even have to leave the house to enjoy spending time together.

Unfortunately, somewhere between becoming a mother, working full-time, and managing our household and special needs family, I forgot how to have fun with my children. Often on family vacations, I was the crazy parent who woke my preschoolers up early so that we could be the first on line to meet the larger than life-sized characters for that all-important photo-op.

From there, we would race to be the first on line waiting for the park to open. As soon as we entered the park, I would pull out the map with my highlighted itinerary so that we could head straight to the best rides and "get them out of the way" before continuing on to the rest of the attractions. In addition, I would insist that my children pose and smile for countless photos to capture these happy moments for future reference in the many photo albums that later sat on our shelves. By the end of the day, as I dragged my exhausted children and rebellious spouse back to the hotel room, I felt exhilarated but they were tired, overloaded, and at times, even hostile.

I can remember when I was outvoted and my family finally insisted on a relaxing vacation that did not include any activities other than sitting near the pool. That is when I learned a very valuable lesson—that the ultimate goal of any family activity is to have fun and the objective is to simply spend time together. Once you realize the benefit of being able to join together in any shared activity, this can be achieved as easily in your own home as on an expensive vacation.

Family time is especially important when you are raising a special needs family. Spending time engaging in activities that everyone can enjoy together helps siblings build a bond that will connect them through the more difficult times. While it may require creativity to find an activity that children of all ages and skills can enjoy together, once they do, they will be delighted to participate and will develop fond memories.

As your children get older, you may even find it enjoyable just relaxing together in the living room, reading books or watching a movie. Though not as exciting as a vacation, being with one another in the same environment, each doing your own thing or pursuing your own interests, can be meaningful. Your children will learn the value of companionship and the support of having someone by your side.

As the relationships between your children develop, they will find more common interests, and enjoy spending time together. Your children will learn to enjoy sitting together as a family, talking to each other about their latest experiences or sharing views on politics and other world events.

Spending quality time together, whether home or away, is an opportunity to make meaningful connections among all family members. Further, it creates cherished memories and an appreciation of each other that forms the foundation on which to build camaraderie that lasts into adulthood.

Summary Points
- Create and carry a bag that contains snacks, a beverage, toys, books, and games to occupy each of your children when you are on the go.
- When planning family gatherings, holidays, or traveling to visit family, discussing expectations and being well prepared will alleviate stress and help avoid conflict or disappointment.
- Although planning family outings can be complicated, the rewards of doing so are worth the effort, resulting in positive bonding time and a break from daily routines.
- There are numerous resources available for special needs families and with some advanced planning your family will be able to create treasured memories to last a lifetime.

- When circumstances dictate, consider hiring outside help or creatively recruit students or people from around your community who can help with babysitting and other support.
- As children with special needs don't have the same attention span as other children, develop a space with activities where your child can keep occupied while the rest of the family is engaged in a meal or other pastime.
- Don't overlook the necessity of quality family bonding time regardless of how and where you spend that time—it serves to enhance relationships between your children.

Part V: Final Thoughts

Chapter 12: Looking Toward the Future

Sooner than you realize, your children suddenly become teenagers and then adults and their lives become their own. Though your children may be far from this stage, it is helpful to be reassured that as your children grow, they will all move on to bigger and better things. They will learn to deal with and establish special relationships with one another. As they mature, daily quarrels about shared attention and space will cease and new issues will arise as they begin to explore the great world outside and separate from the family. For the child with special needs, there will be issues of ending the security of a daily school schedule and finding a suitable adult program. Some will be moving out of their parents' home and will have to face the reality of living with other people.

As they begin to pursue a life on their own, many siblings continue to feel the bond with their brother or sister with special needs and feel guilty about moving away from or without them. Many siblings worry about their parents, too, and the continued challenges they will face in caring for the child with special needs. These siblings face all of the challenges that other people their age face, such as finding a rewarding career, a suitable mate and the financial independence to support a family, but they are still tied to their family of origin.

The independence, confidence, and resourcefulness you instill in each of your children, will go a long way in preparing them for these life challenges. Hopefully, all of the important lessons they learned about forming strong relationships and being there for others will help them to face each of the new roles they take on with strength and commitment.

Future Milestones and Transitions

All children face challenges and life transitions as they mature, but those who are part of special needs family, may be better prepared to deal with and navigate their way through them. Many of the milestones and experiences they will face include the following:

- **Life is Unpredictable and Ever-Changing**
  As they become adults, your children enter the world knowing that life is something that happens beyond their control, and it is their responsibility to make it the best it can be. Unlike their peers who may have an expectation that if they do well in school and strive to achieve their vocational goals their life will go as planned, your children will enter the adult world with a much more realistic view that nothing in life is guaranteed. They are more mature about pursuing their life goals. Many pursue careers that allow them to help other people, including those with special needs. Many become medical and mental health professionals with a remarkable capacity to empathize with the families, and especially the siblings of the people they encounter professionally.

- **Preparing for Separation from the Family**
  The concerns that siblings have for their brother or sister with special needs do not end once they leave the house. Many choose to remain involved and have a desire to become guardians and caregivers when their parents can no longer provide care. Brothers and sisters should share equally in this responsibility. Depending on where you live and the services that are available, it may be more difficult to care for an individual with special needs once they leave the structure of the school system and enter into the system of adult services. Often the siblings are acutely aware of the emotional and financial burden that falls on their parents in caring for their sibling, especially as their parents are aging and may become unable to ad-

equately care for the adult child with special needs. In some cases, the siblings are left to take care of their parents *and* the sibling with special needs. This decision should come from the siblings rather than from their parents, and they must be willing to assume the primary responsibility of caring for their brother or sister once their parents are no longer able to do so.

- **Becoming Parents**
  Your children may eventually have concerns about the responsibilities of caring for their own families knowing that they will always have a connection to and some responsibility toward caring for their sibling. They should be reminded of what they learned as they were growing up—being patient, compassionate, and caring—and know that they are well suited for the responsibilities that lie ahead. As a parent, I can appreciate the opportunity to watch my adult children develop into confident and competent parents themselves. There is no greater pay off than the knowledge that my grandchildren are the true beneficiaries of all of our hard work!

- **Making the World a Better Place**
  Many adults have a strong desire to advocate for their sibling and for other people with special needs. They have seen first hand the obstacles that their siblings faced and are aware of the discrimination that continues to exist toward individuals with special needs. They are familiar with the many challenges their parents had to overcome in trying to get services and programs for their sibling and they are eager to remove some of those obstacles for other families, especially those that are just starting out.

- **Possible Feelings of Guilt**

  People with special needs often share the fact that they rely on their brothers and sisters for social contact because they have few friends and other sources of social support. These siblings may feel guilty that they have moved on while their sibling with special needs still lives in their parents' home or that they have achieved their vocational goals while their sibling has not. It is important to acknowledge these feelings, rather than avoiding them so that the feelings can be properly addressed and don't evolve into something deeper or impair other relationships.

- **Unconditional Love and Support**

  Your children will continue to love and support their brother or sister with special needs, even if from a distance, as they move on with their lives. They are aware of the unconditional love and support that their sibling has for them—and in fact that all the siblings have for each other—which sets a stable, emotional foundation. Many siblings reach out to their brother or sister with special needs through regular phone calls or visits and this type of contact should be praised and encouraged.

Thoughts For All Parents to Consider

For those parents who require intermittent reinforcement of the important messages of this book, here are a few takeaway points that you may want to reread frequently or post somewhere in your home.

1. **Recognize the diversity in your children and promote it.**
   Whether you are engaging in a group or individual activity, it is essential to allow each of your children the time and opportunity to develop their own talents and to be recognized for their strengths.

2. **Don't wait for Thanksgiving to say thank you.**

   Be sure to demonstrate appreciation when your three-year-old puts toys away, your teenager helps unpack the groceries or your child with special needs sets the dinner table. Saying thank you doesn't cost anything and its impact can be invaluable. You will help your children feel appreciated and encourage them to acknowledge all of the other important people in their life by saying thank you, as well. Take time to thank your partner and be gracious in accepting thanks from others.

3. **Be open to making compromises or acknowledge when another makes a sacrifice to help you.**

   Whether it is an issue with your spouse or between your children, don't give up on the negotiations. You may want to suggest taking a break but be sure to revisit the issue because if it is not resolved it will resurface. Do your best, and encourage others, to find a way to make compromises that will work for all parties.

4. **Communication is essential.**

   Be available to listen and be open about your feelings. Encourage your partner and children to do the same. If you find that someone is experiencing a difficult time, try to help the person put his or her feelings into words. Creating a script that can be used to convey certain feelings and shared experiences will go a long way in helping you and your children express yourselves, especially during the most stressful times.

5. **Get support when needed.**

   Create a support system that allows you to have special moments with your children or with your spouse and to take a time out when you need a break. Accept help from family and friends when offered and don't be ashamed to ask for help when needed. If necessary, pay for extra help when you need it or find volunteers that are willing to give you a hand.

6. **Find ways to strengthen yourself through the hard times.**
Be open to trying new things and don't feel discouraged when they don't work out. Give yourself a break and know when you need one. Give yourself praise when you overcome an obstacle, resolve a problem, or achieve any small success.

7. **Maintain your sense of humor and have fun.**
As you find the positive or the humor in even the most difficult times, you will feel better and your children will begin to view the world in a more positive way. Being surrounded by positive people will also motivate you to see the good that can exist in your life.

Finding and Keeping the Faith

Having faith provides a person with a great deal of support. Whether it is the source of comfort that you receive from those who are a part of your religious group or the belief that there is good in the world, your belief system becomes a source of great comfort.

Faith is up to you. It doesn't necessarily have to involve a God but rather the acceptance and belief in your ability to overcome the challenges and obstacles you face.

Faith requires you to relinquish your cognitive and emotional connection to the situation. The reality is that there are so many aspects of your life that are outside of your influence or control. But you can control the happiness in your life and you can help your children to find happiness in their lives.

Life may be a roller coaster but we can learn to enjoy the ride. This analogy is especially relevant for me because I don't like roller coasters and tend to steer toward the slower and easier rides at an amusement park. But having faith helps me adapt to the ride, with all its ups and downs, and that makes my life much easier.

My faith helps me believe that children with special needs are created with a purpose. I believe that they are a part of our life because they help us to appreciate all that we have. They teach us that we are capable of doing far more than we can imagine. They give us the strength to get through difficult times and to appreciate the blessings that exist in our life.

Turning Negatives to Positives

Developing a positive outlook becomes an active process that you and your family can engage in together. This is not to suggest that you rely on denial or use repression to push the feelings out of your consciousness. Rather, you accept your negative feelings and decide actively to replace them with something that is positive.

Once you believe in your ability to determine the outcome for your family, you will become empowered. Your happiness and that of your family requires effort and you must decide to strive for it, every day. You must look into yourself and into the faces of your children and find the happiness that exists.

Keeping the happiness and using positive affirmations to confirm the existence of something that is positive, helps you teach your children to strive for and achieve their own happiness.

In the world of a special needs family, it is easy to see the pitfalls. It is easy to find reasons to feel bad. It is easy to feel sorry for yourself. You must work that much harder to see the good in your situation.

As you make the effort to find pleasure and satisfaction in your life, don't be fake or unreal about your happiness. You really won't be able to fool anyone, especially your children, who will be able to see right through that facade.

Believe that something beneficial will occur and be brave enough to endure the process that it will take to experience the good. You will discover that it is worth the wait and the future will look better and brighter.

There are immediate benefits to facing your life in this way. As you reevaluate your situation, you will find something positive in each of your children. You may not be able to make it better for yourself or for your children but you can make them into better people.

Acceptance involves the recognition that everyone is different yet special in some way. The true challenge is not in taking care of a child with special needs, it is in finding the special qualities that makes that child unique.

When our children are born, they hold enormous hope and potential. We are eager to see the color of their eyes and feel the texture of their hair. But, we have as much interest in watching how their personalities develop.

To find this hope, we must first recognize that some children with special needs do not have the ability to achieve success that is based on the standards that we set for them. Some children do not develop a level of independence that allows them to function separately from their parents. But those children have strengths that we do not possess.

The main lesson we learn from rearing a child with special needs and his or her siblings is to love each child unconditionally. We learn that our focus should be on personal attributes rather than achievements.

Learning to love a child with special needs is the purest form of love. These children teach us what love should be. The love they share with us is authentic and they do not expect anything in return.

It isn't hard to love our son because he has the most beautiful smile, adorable dimples, and amazing deep blue eyes. But, beyond these beautiful features, he has a special soul. He is a child that we often refer to as an angel.

He is always content and cheerful. From the moment that he gets up in the morning to the time that he goes to bed at night, he always has a smile on his face. He has a good sense of humor and says many funny things. He is never depressed or sad. He is happiest when he sees other people who are happy. He is truly pained when he sees someone who is sad.

Children with special needs possess an astute sense and awareness of the world around them. They enter this world free from evil and sin and do not have, nor develop bad thoughts about other people. This is, perhaps, the quality that makes them so special and unique.

The Silver Lining

The silver lining for children in a special needs family is that they learn to value everyone, including themselves, regardless of their abilities. Teaching your children to see the beauty in others will help them learn to appreciate themselves. Teaching them compassion and to place value in their relationships will help your children feel more confident about themselves.

The siblings in a special needs family appreciate all that they have and all that they can do, rather than focusing on wanting more. They learn that love is not based on their achievements. They do not rely on others to help them feel fulfilled. They feel fulfilled because they can care for themselves and for others. And, as a result, they develop good character. They learn that they have a greater ability to overcome their own challenges than they believed.

They also learn not to feel sorry for their sibling—or any other person with special needs—but rather, to feel warmly toward them. They learn to engage people with difference in their lives. In sharing themselves with others, they experience compassion and fulfillment in a much deeper way.

The Greatest Gift

Whenever possible, believe that every day is a gift. Sometimes that gift may come in the most unexpected and surprising packages.

Make the most of every day because life is just too short.

Once you have this outlook, you can take the time to stop and smell the roses.

You can laugh at your child when he says something funny. You will better appreciate the love and support that your partner shows, even in the slightest way.

Appreciate what each day has to offer. The day may not be perfect and life may not be as planned, but each moment has the potential to give you a good feeling. Each opportunity gives you the potential to accomplish something you haven't yet achieved. Each relationship you develop gives you the potential to do something for someone else that makes you and them feel better.

You have to love yourself before you can love others. It is important to be able to identify those characteristics that you appreciate in yourself and to feel good about yourself before you can love someone else. If you are looking to your children or to your spouse for that confirmation, then you are creating a barrier in the relationship and you can't give them your full heart. But when you know all that you have to offer, your self-esteem will blossom and your love will have no bounds.

You should focus on building your self-esteem not through being a good parent, good spouse, or good worker, but rather through being a good person. Once you value yourself, you can teach your children to value who they are.

Embrace the challenges. Life is tough but so are you. Once you have gotten through a challenge, confirm your belief in yourself. This will empower you to face similar challenges in the future.

The future may not be as planned but there will most assuredly be a future. Acceptance will help you to value each happy moment that you are fortunate to share with your family. The unique bond and love that exists because you are a special needs family will help you live a more satisfying life. And, as long you maintain an open mind and an open heart, everything will work out for the best.

Summary Points

- Once children grow up to become young adults they will face many milestones and transitions, some exciting but some challenging. These include separation, facing the unknown, entering into relationships and becoming parents, contributing to the world, and concerns about family and siblings. Being aware of these challenges can help you to help them navigate these life changes.
- Children are diverse regardless of limitations.
- Make compromises, express gratitude, and keep the lines of communication open between all family members, even when they live far from home.
- Maintain a sense of humor and laugh as often as you can together with your family.
- Know that it is not a sign of weakness to ask for help or support when needed.
- Always have faith that things will work out for the best.
- Look for the silver lining and the positive aspects of life.
- Remember, your children are a gift that will expand and enrich your life, but don't rely on them to define who you are.

Epilogue: Finding Our Family's Silver Lining

As I accepted having a child with special needs, I opened my eyes and heart to the many things in my life for which I am thankful. I could not imagine living my life without our son being a part of it.

As I look into Jonathan's deep blue eyes and see his bright smile, I wonder how different my life would be if he did not have special needs. I dream about the friendships he might have and the many achievements we could have shared.

But at the same time, I know that he is a happy and content young man who feels love and shares love. I know that he has helped me to become a stronger and better person and for that I am forever grateful.

Acceptance for me involved a belief system. Though I am a religious person and believe that a higher power controls my destiny, this was not a religious matter. My belief was that although I do not control my own destiny and certainly may not be able to understand my situation, I must accept my destiny and appreciate the unknown.

Acceptance meant that though I may not be able to explain or tolerate everything I am experiencing at the present time, I am willing to look toward the future and find the good.

Acceptance allowed me to move past the anger and forgive myself for all that I could not fix or control.

And as a family, we accepted our mission to create the best life we could with the strengths and abilities that we were given. As a result, we truly feel blessed that Jonathan is in our life.

One of the most recognizable blessings is that he has taught us to be caring and thoughtful. He has taught us not to focus on the hardships, but to seek out the good. He has taught us to laugh more and to value each experience.

We have all learned to identify and embrace those characteristics that make each family member different and unique. We have all learned to value our relationships and the love we have to share with one another.

As parents of a child with special needs, we have developed a natural instinct to love and protect each of our children. Jonathan has taught us to value and respect him, and has taught us to find and appreciate the characteristics that make each of our children unique. He has taught us to appreciate his heartwarming laugh and love for life, and has given us a greater capacity to love and value all our children.

As you travel along this special road, I hope you too will find your silver lining and raise enlightened children who will make the world a richer place.

Acknowledgments

To our parents, of blessed memory, who have provided the foundation that helped us endure the toughest times. Thanks, first to my parents, Elias and Ilse Lauer for giving me the confidence to believe in myself and for showing me how to become a loving parent. You gave me every opportunity to achieve my professional goals and exemplified the importance of being a good person. Because of your strength, I believe that there is nothing that I cannot achieve if I put my heart and mind to it. There isn't a day that goes by that I don't think of you and wish you were here to share the pride I have for all that my children have accomplished. To my in-laws, Joseph and Elsie Listhaus, thank you for raising such a confident and determined son who learned from his parents who were Holocaust survivors that no obstacle is insurmountable and that every day is another opportunity to count your blessings. You raised a very good son and brother but an even better father and husband.

To our caring siblings, Harry, Beverly, Simmy, Ruth, Chaim, Michelle, Aaron, Cindy, Avi and Aleeza who showed us the value of a sibling's love and supported us in too many ways to mention. You are always there for us and for our children and we couldn't do it without you!

To Talia Rosenblatt-Cohen for helping me through the very early, and very complicated, initial stages of the writing process and to her grandmother, a very dear friend, Mrs. Esther Rosenblatt, of blessed memory, for introducing us.

Thank you to Robert Schneider for capturing many of our family's most cherished moments, and for taking my photo for the book, and to

Mara Simon and Levi Grossbaum for adding their special touches to the cover.

Special thanks to June Clark for helping to organize my thoughts into a more cohesive, user-friendly manuscript. Thank you for the frequent reminders that my message was important to share and for helping me stay on course despite the many distractions.

I am grateful to those who agreed to review early drafts, especially Dan Paisner and Charles Salzberg, and to those who helped with the final editing, Barbara Gottfried and Gwen Francis. I truly appreciate your attention to detail and your encouragement to persevere despite all of the revisions.

Thank you to our many incredible friends and our entire support team for your advice and actions, big and small. Each of you contributed in a meaningful way and I apologize if I was too busy at times to thank you.

As a family, we thank our dear friends, Seryl and Charles Kushner, who helped create the unique school environment that allowed Jonathan and his peers to feel included. Your special relationship with Jonathan and your belief that all children deserve the opportunity to receive the individualized education that will help them learn had an invaluable impact on our family and our community.

Certain stories included in this book have come from remarks and observations from patients, family, friends, colleagues, and acquaintances I met over the years. If something sounds familiar, I hope that a collective thank you, or apology, will be sufficient.

My gratitude begins and ends with my loving husband, Alan, who has been a primary source of strength for me since the day we met. We became parents for the first time together and have become better parents each and every day because of the life we share. I couldn't have asked for a better father for my children! You put your family first and give us everything you have every single day. Most of all, you are energized by our achievements and that pushes us to do more. May we continue to share our blessed life in good health and maintain our sense of humor so that we can enjoy it!

To our four incredible and very special children, Joe, Jason, Jonathan and Jessica whose love for one another inspired me to share our story. I am so fortunate to be your parent, and to have seen you find your individual strengths and accept your differences. I hope that you are blessed to achieve your dreams with the gifts that God has given you. I cherish each of the special moments we share, individually and as a group, and look forward to creating many more memories together. And finally, thank you Maggie for enriching our family by becoming one of our children and for giving us our greatest blessings, Henry and Kailey.